The Tunnel Under tl

Thomas Whiteside

Alpha Editions

This edition published in 2024

ISBN : 9789362517951

Design and Setting By
Alpha Editions
www.alphaedis.com
Email - info@alphaedis.com

As per information held with us this book is in Public Domain.
This book is a reproduction of an important historical work. Alpha Editions uses the best technology to reproduce historical work in the same manner it was first published to preserve its original nature. Any marks or number seen are left intentionally to preserve its true form.

Contents

One .... - 1 -
Two .... - 7 -
Three .... - 29 -
Four .... - 47 -
Five .... - 68 -

One

IN THE SOCIAL HISTORY of England, the English Channel, that proud sea passage some three hundred and fifty miles long, has separated that country from the Continent as by a great gulf or a bottomless chasm. However, at its narrowest point, between Dover and Cap Gris-Nez—a distance of some twenty-one and a half miles—the Channel, despite any impression that storm-tossed sea travelers across it may have of yawning profundities below, is actually a body of water shaped less like a marine chasm than like an extremely shallow puddle. Indeed, the relationship of depth to breadth across the Strait of Dover is quite extraordinary, being as one to five hundred. This relationship can perhaps be most graphically illustrated by drawing a section profile of the Channel to scale. If the drawing were two feet long, the straight line representing the level of the sea and the line representing the profile of the Channel bottom would be so close together as to be barely distinguishable from one another. At its narrowest part, the Channel is nowhere more than two hundred and sixteen feet deep, and for half of the distance across, it is less than a hundred feet deep. It is just this extreme shallowness, in combination with strong winds] and tidal currents flowing in the Channel neck between the North Sea and the Atlantic, that makes the seas of the Strait of Dover so formidable, especially in the winter months. The weather is so bad during November and December that the odds of a gale's occurring on any given day are computed by the marine signal station at Dunkirk at one in seven, and during the whole year there are only sixty periods in which the weather remains decent in the Channel through a whole day. Under these difficult conditions, the passage of people traveling across the Channel by ferry between England and France is a notoriously trying one; the experience has been mentioned in print during the last hundred years in such phrases as "that fearful ordeal," "an hour and a half's torture," and "that unspeakable horror." Writing in the *Revue des Deux Mondes* in 1882, a French writer named Valbert described the trip from Dover to Calais as "two centuries ... of agony." Ninety-odd years ago, an article dealing with the Channel passage, in *The Gentleman's Magazine*, asserted that hundreds of thousands of people crossing the Strait each year suffered in a manner that beggared description. "Probably there is no other piece of travelling in civilized countries, where, within equal times, so much suffering is endured; certainly it would be hard to find another voyage of equal length which is so much feared," the author said, and he went on to report that only one day out of four was calm, on the average, while about three days in every eight were made dreadful to passengers by heavy weather. He concluded, with feeling, "What wonder that, under such circumstances, patriotism often fails to survive; and that if any wish is felt in mid-Channel, it is that, after all, England was not an island."

How many Englishmen, their loyalty having been subjected to this strain, might express the same wish upon safely gaining high ground again is a question the writer in *The Gentleman's Magazine* did not venture to discuss. However, there is no question about the persistence with which, during the past century at least, cross-Channel ferry passengers have spoken about or written about the desirability of some sort of dry-land passage between England and France. Engineers have been attracted to the idea of constructing such a passage for at least a hundred and fifty years. During that time, they have come up with proposals for crossing the Channel by spanning it with great bridges, by laying down submersible tubes resting on the sea bottom or floating halfway between sea bed and sea level, or even by using transports shaped like enormous tea wagons, whose wheels would travel along rails below sea level and whose platforms would tower high above the highest waves. But more commonly than by any other means, they have proposed to do away with the hazards and hardships of the Channel boat crossing by boring a traffic tunnel under the rock strata that lie at conveniently shallow depths under sea level. The idea of a Channel tunnel, at once abolishing seasickness and connecting England with the Continent by an easy arterial flow of goods and travelers, always has had about it a quality of grand simplicity—the simplicity of a very large extension of an easily comprehended principle; in this case, digging a hole—that has proved irresistible in appeal to generations not only of engineers but of visionaries and promoters of all kinds.

The tunnel seems always to have had a capacity to arouse in its proponents a peculiarly passionate and unquenchable enthusiasm. Men have devoted their adult lives to promoting the cause of the tunnel, and such a powerful grip does the project seem to have had on the imagination of its various designers that just to look at some of their old drawings—depicting, for example, down to the finest detail of architectural ornamentation, ventilation stations for the tunnel sticking out of the surface of the Channel as ships sail gracefully about nearby—one might almost think that the tunnel was an accomplished reality, and the artist merely a conscientious reporter of an existing scene. Such is the minute detail in which the tunnel has been designed by various people that eighty-six years ago the French Assembly approved a tunnel bill that specified the price of railway tickets for the Channel-tunnel journey, and even contained a clause requiring second-class carriages to be provided with stuffed seats rather than the harder accommodations provided for third-class passengers. And an Englishman called William Collard, who died in 1943, after occupying himself for thirty years with the problem of the Channel tunnel, in 1928 wrote and published a book on the subject that went so far as to work out a time-table for Channel-tunnel trains between Paris and London, complete with train and platform numbers and arrival and departure times at intermediate stations in Kent and northern France. As for the actual engineering details, a Channel tunnel has been the subject of studies that have ranged from collections of mere rough guesses to the most elaborate engineering, geological, and hydrographic surveys carried out by highly competent civil-engineering companies. Interestingly enough, ever since the days, a century or so ago, when practical Victorian engineers began taking up the problem, the technical feasibility of constructing a tunnel under the Channel has never really been seriously questioned. Yet, despite effort piled on effort and campaign mounted on campaign, over all the years, by engineers, politicians, and promoters, nobody has quite been able to push the project through. Up to now, every time the proponents of a tunnel have tried to advance the scheme, they have encountered a difficulty harder to understand, harder to identify, and, indeed, harder to break through than any rock stratum.

The difficulty seems to lie in the degree to which, among Englishmen, the Channel has been not only a body of water but a state of mind. Because of the prevalence of this curious force, the history of the scheme to put a tunnel below the Channel has proved almost as stormy as the Channel waves themselves. Winston Churchill, in an article in the London *Daily Mail*, wrote in 1936, "There are few projects against which there exists a deeper and more enduring prejudice than the construction of a railway tunnel between Dover and Calais. Again and again it has been brought forward under powerful and influential sponsorship. Again and again it has been prevented." Mr. Churchill, who could never be accused of lacking understanding of the British character, was obliged to add that he found the resistance to the tunnel "a mystery." Some thirty-five times between 1882 and 1950 the subject of the Channel tunnel was brought before Parliament in one form or another for discussion, and ten bills on behalf of the project have been rejected or set aside. On several occasions, the Parliamentary vote on the tunnel has been close enough to bring the tunnel within reach of becoming a reality, and in the eighties the construction of pilot tunnels for a distance under the sea from the English and French coasts was even started. But always the tunnel advocates have had to give way before persistent opposition, and always they have had to begin their exertions all over again. Successive generations of Englishmen have argued with each other—and with the French, who have never showed any opposition to a Channel tunnel—with considerable vehemence. The ranks of pro-tunnel people have included Sir Winston Churchill (who once called the British opposition to the tunnel "occult"), Prince Albert, and, at one point, Queen Victoria; and the people publicly lining themselves up with the anti-tunnel forces have included Lord Randolph Churchill (Sir Winston's father), Alfred, Lord

Tennyson, Robert Browning, Professor Thomas Huxley, and, more recently, First Viscount Montgomery of Alamein. Queen Victoria, once pro-tunnel, later turned anti-tunnel; her sometime Prime Minister, William E. Gladstone, took an anti-tunnel position at one period when he was in office, and later, out of it, turned pro-tunnel. Throughout its stormy history the tunnel project has had the qualities of fantasy and nightmare—a thing of airy grace and claustrophobic horror; a long, bright kaleidoscope of promoters' promises and a cavern resounding with Cyclopean bellowing. Proponents of the tunnel have called it an end to seasickness, a boon to peace, international understanding, and trade; and they have hailed it as potentially the greatest civil-engineering feat of their particular century. Its opponents have referred to it sharply as "a mischievous project," and they have denounced it as a military menace that would have enabled the French (or Germans) to use it as a means of invading England—the thought of which, in 1914, caused one prominent English anti-tunneler, Admiral Sir Algernon de Horsey, publicly to characterize as "unworthy of consideration" the dissenting views of pro-tunnelers, whom he contemptuously referred to as "those poor creatures who have no stomach for an hour's sea passage, and who think retention of their dinners more important than the safety of their country." Over the years, anti-tunnel forces have used as ammunition an extraordinary variety of further arguments, which have ranged from objections about probable customs difficulties at the English and French ends of the tunnel to suspicions that a Channel tunnel would make it easier for international Socialists to commingle and conspire.

Behind all these given reasons, no matter how elaborate or how special they might be, there has always lurked something else, a consideration more subtle, more elusive, more profound, and less answer able than any specific objections to the construction of a Channel tunnel—the consideration of England's traditional insular position, the feeling that somehow, if England were to be connected by a tunnel with the Continent, the peculiar meaning, to an Englishman, of being English would never be quite the same again. It is this feeling, no doubt, that in 1882 motivated an article on the tunnel, in so sober a publication as *The Solicitors' Journal*, to express about it an uneasiness bordering on alarm, on the ground that, if successful, the construction of a tunnel would "effect a change in the natural geographical condition of things." And it is no doubt something of the same feeling that prompted Lord Randolph Churchill, during a speech attacking a bill for a Channel tunnel before the House of Commons in 1889—the bill was defeated, of course—to observe skillfully that "the reputation of England has hitherto depended upon her being, as it were, *virgo intacta*."

If the proponents and promoters of the tunnel have never quite succeeded in putting their project across in all the years, they have never quite given up trying, either; and now, in a new strategic era of nuclear rockets, a new era of transport in which air ferries to the Continent carry cars as well as passengers, and a new era of trade, marked by the emergence and successful growth of the European Economic Community, or Common Market, the pro-tunnel forces have been at it again, in what one of the leading pro-tunnelers has called "a last glorious effort to get this thing through." This time they have encountered what they consider to be the most encouraging kind of progress in the entire history of the scheme. In April, 1960, an organization called the Channel Tunnel Study Group announced, in London, a new series of proposals for a Channel tunnel, based on a number of recent elaborate studies on the subject. The proposals called for twin parallel all-electric railway tunnels, either bored or immersed, with trains that would carry passengers and transport, in piggyback fashion, cars, buses, and trucks. The double tunnel, if of the immersed kind, would be 26 miles long between portals. A bored tunnel, as planned, would be 32 miles long and would be by far the longest traffic tunnel of either the underwater or under-mountain variety in the world. The longest continuous subaqueous traffic tunnel in existence is the rail tunnel under the Mersey, connecting Liverpool and Birkenhead, a distance of 2.2 miles; the longest rail tunnel through a mountain is the Simplon Tunnel, 12.3 miles in length. The Channel tunnel would run between the areas of Sangatte and Calais on the French side, and between Ashford and Folkestone on the English side. Trains would travel through it at an average speed of 65 miles an hour, reaching 87 miles an hour in some places, and at rush hours they would be capable of running 4,200 passengers and 1,800 vehicles on flatcars every hour in each direction. While a true vehicular tunnel could also be constructed, the obviously tremendous problems of keeping it safely ventilated at present make this particular project, according to the engineers, prohibitively expensive to build and maintain. The train journey from London to Paris via the proposed tunnel would take four hours and twenty minutes; the passenger trains would pass through the tunnel in about thirty minutes. Passengers would pay 32 shillings, or $4.48–$2.92 cheaper than the cost of a first-class passenger ticket on the Dover-Calais sea-ferry—to ride through the tunnel; the cost of accompanied small cars would be $16.48, a claimed 30 per cent less than a comparable sea-ferry charge. The tunnel would take four to five years to build, and the Study Group estimated that, including the rail terminals at both ends, it would cost approximately $364,000,000.

All that the Study Group, which represents British, French and American commercial interests, needs to go ahead with the project and turn it into a reality is—besides money, and the Study Group seems to be confident that it can attract that—the approval of the British and French Governments of the scheme. For all practical purposes, the French Government never has had any objection to a fixed installation linking both sides of the Channel, and as far as the official British attitude is concerned, when the British Government announced, in July, 1961, that it would seek full membership in the European Common Market, most of the tunnel people felt sure that the forces of British insularity which had hindered the development of a tunnel for nearly a century at last had been dealt a blow to make them reel. But what raised the pro-tunnelers' excitement to the greatest pitch of all was the decision of the French and British Governments, last October, to hold discussions on the problem of building either a bridge or a tunnel. When these discussions got under way last November, the main question before the negotiators was the economic practicality of such a huge undertaking.

Yet, with all the encouragement, few of the pro-tunnelers in England seem willing to make a flat prediction that the British Government will actively support the construction of a tunnel. They have been disappointed too often. Then again, despite the generally high hopes that this time the old strategic objections to the construction of a tunnel have been pretty well forgotten, pro-tunnelers are well aware that a number of Englishmen with vivid memories of 1940 are still doubtful about the project. "The Channel saved us last time, even in the age of the airplane, didn't it?" one English barrister said a while ago, in talking of his feelings about building the Channel tunnel. The tunnel project has the open enmity of Viscount Montgomery, who has made repeated attacks on it and who in 1960 demanded, in a newspaper interview, that before the Government took any stand on behalf of such a project, "The British people as a whole should be consulted and vote on the Channel tunnel as part of a General-Elections program." And, to show that the spirit of the anti-tunnelers has not lost its resilience, Major-General Sir Edward L. Spears, in the correspondence columns of the London *Times* in April of that same year, denounced the latest Channel-tunnel scheme as "a plan which will not only cost millions of public money, but will let loose on to our inadequate roads eighteen hundred more vehicles an hour, each driven by a right-of-the-road driver in a machine whose steering wheel is on the left."

Two

THE FIRST SCHEME for the construction of a tunnel beneath the English Channel was put forward in France, in 1802, by a mining engineer named Albert Mathieu, who that year displayed plans for such a work in Paris, at the Palais du Luxembourg and the École Nationale Supérieure des Mines. Mathieu's tunnel, divided into two lengths totaling about eighteen and a half miles, was to be illuminated by oil lamps and ventilated at intervals by chimneys projecting above the sea into the open air, and its base was to be a paved way over which relays of horses would gallop, pulling coachloads of passengers and mail between France and England in a couple of hours or so of actual traveling time, with changes of horses being provided at an artificial island to be constructed in mid-Channel. Mathieu managed to have his project brought to the attention of Napoleon Bonaparte, the First Consul, who was sufficiently impressed with it to bring it to the attention of Charles James Fox during a personal meeting of the two men during the Peace of Amiens. Fox described it as "one of the great enterprises we can now undertake together." But the project got no further than this talking stage. In 1803, a Frenchman named de Mottray came up with another proposal for creating a passage underneath the Channel. It consisted of laying down sections of a long, submerged tube on top of the sea bed between England and France, the sections being linked together in such a way as to form a watertight tunnel. However, Mottray's project petered out quickly, too, and the subject of an undersea connection between the two countries lay dormant until 1833, when it attracted the attention of a man named Aimé Thomé de Gamond, a twenty-six-year-old French civil engineer and hydrographer of visionary inclinations.

Thomé de Gamond was to turn into an incomparably zealous and persistent projector of ways in which people could cross between England and France without getting wet or seasick; he devoted himself to the problem for no less than thirty-four years, and had no hesitation in exposing himself to extraordinary physical dangers in the course of his researches. Unlike the plans of his predecessors, Thomé de Gamond's were based upon fairly systematic hydrographic or geological surveys of the Channel area. In 1833 he made the first of these surveys by taking marine soundings to establish a profile of the sea bottom in a line between Calais and Dover; on the basis of this, he drew up, in 1834, a plan for a submerged iron tube that was to be laid down in prefabricated sections on the bed of the Strait of Dover and then lined with masonry, the irregular bottom of the sea meanwhile having been prepared to receive the tube through the leveling action of a great battering-ram and rake operated from the surface by boat. By 1835, Thomé de Gamond modified this scheme by eliminating the prefabricated tube in favor of a movable hydrographic shield that would slowly advance across the Channel bottom, leaving a masonry tube behind it as it progressed. But the rate of progress, he calculated, would be slow; the work was to take thirty years to complete, or fifteen years if work began on two shores simultaneously. Thomé de Gamond moved on to schemes for other ways of crossing the Channel, and between 1835 and 1836 he turned out, successively, detailed plans for five types of cross-Channel bridges. They included a granite-and-steel bridge of colossal proportions, and with arches "higher than the cupola of St. Paul's, London," which was to be built between Ness Corner Point and Calais; a flat-bottomed steam-driven concrete-and-stone ferryboat, of such size as to constitute "a true floating island," which would travel between two great piers each jutting out five miles into the Channel between Ness Corner Point and Cap Blanc-Nez; and a massive artificial isthmus of stone, which would stretch from Cap Gris-Nez to Dover and block the neck of the English Channel except for three transverse cuttings spanned by movable bridges, which Thomé de Gamond allowed across his work for the passage of ships. Thomé de Gamond was particularly fond of his isthmus scheme. He traveled to London and there promoted it vigorously among interested Englishmen during the Universal Exhibition of 1851, but he reluctantly abandoned it because of objections to its high estimated cost of £33,600,000 and to what he described as "the obstinate resistance of mariners, who objected to their being obliged to ply their ships through the narrow channels."

Such exasperating objections to joining England and France above water sent Thomé de Gamond back to the idea of doing the job under the sea, and between 1842 and 1855 he made various energetic explorations of the Channel area in an attempt to determine the feasibility of driving a tunnel through the rock formations under the Strait. Geological conditions existing in the middle of the Strait were, up to that time, almost entirely a matter of surmise, based on observations made on the British and French sides of the Channel, and in the process of finding out more about them, Thomé de Gamond decided to descend in person to the bottom of the Channel to collect geological specimens. In 1855, at the age of forty-eight, he had the hardihood to make a number of such descents, unencumbered by diving equipment, in the middle of the Strait. Naked except for wrappings that he wound about his head to keep in place pads of buttered lint he had plastered over his ears, to protect them from high water pressure, he would plunge to the bottom of the Channel, weighted down by bags of flints and trailing a long safety line attached to his body, and a red distress line attached to his left arm, from a rowboat occupied also by a Channel pilot, a young assistant, and his own daughter, who went along to keep watch over him. On the deepest of these descents, at a point off Folkestone, Thomé de Gamond, having put a spoonful of olive oil into his mouth as a lubricant that would allow him to expel air from his lungs without permitting water at high pressure to force its way in, dived down weighted by four bags of flints weighing a total of 180 pounds. About his waist he wore a belt of ten inflated pig's bladders, which were to pull him rapidly to the surface after he had scooped up his geological specimen from the Channel bed and released his ballast, and, using this system, he actually touched bottom at a depth of between 99 and 108 feet. His ascent from this particular dive was not unremarkable, either; in an account of it, he wrote that just after he had left the bottom of the Channel with a sample of clay

> ... I was attacked by voracious fish, which seized me by the legs and arms. One of them bit me on the chin, and would at the same time have attacked my throat if it had not been preserved by a thick handkerchief.... I was fortunate enough not to open my mouth, and I reappeared on top of the water after being immersed fifty-two seconds. My men saw one of the monsters which had assailed me, and which did not leave me until I had reached the surface. They were conger eels.

Thomé de Gamond's geological observations, although they were certainly sketchy by later standards, were enough to convince him of the feasibility of a mined tunnel under the Channel, and in 1856 he drew up plans for such a work. This was to be a stone affair containing a double set of railroad tracks. It was to stretch twenty-one miles, from Cap Gris-Nez to Eastwear Point, and from these places was to connect, by more than nine miles at each end of sloping access tunnels, with the French and British railway systems. The junctions of the sloping access tunnels and the main tunnel itself were to be marked by wide shafts, about three hundred feet deep, at the bottom of which travelers would encounter the frontier stations of each nation. The line of the main tunnel was to be marked above the surface by a series of twelve small artificial islands made of stone. These were to be surmounted with lighthouses and were to contain ventilating shafts connecting with the tunnel. Thomé de Gamond prudently provided the ventilation shafts in his plans with sea valves, so that in case of war between England and France each nation would have the opportunity of flooding the tunnel on short notice. The tunnel was designed to cross the northern tip of the Varne, a narrow, submerged shelf that lies parallel to the English coast about ten miles off Folkestone, and so close to the surface that at low tide it is only about fifteen feet under water at its highest point. Thomé de Gamond planned to raise the Varne above water level, thus converting it into an artificial island, by building it up with rocks and earth brought to the spot in ships. Through this earth, engineers would dig a great shaft down to the level of the tunnel, so that the horizontal mining of the tunnel as a whole could be carried on from four working faces simultaneously, instead of only two. The great shaft was also to serve as a means of ventilating the tunnel and communicating with it from the outside, and around its apex Thomé de Gamond planned, with a characteristically grand flourish, an international port called the Étoile de Varne, which was to have four outer quays and an interior harbor, as well as amenities such as living quarters for personnel and a first-class lighthouse. As for the shaft leading down to the railway tunnel, according to alternate versions of Thomé de Gamond's plan, it was to be at least 350 feet—and possibly as much as 984 feet—in diameter, and 147 feet deep; and, according to a contemporary account in the Paris newspaper *La Patrie*, "an open station [would be] formed as spacious as the court of the Louvre, where travelers might halt to take air after running a quarter of an hour under the bottom of the Strait."

From the bottom of this deep station, trains might also ascend by means of gently spiraling ramps to the surface of the Étoile de Varne, *La Patrie* reported. The newspaper went on to invite its readers to contemplate the panorama at sea level:

> Imagine a train full of travelers, after having run for fifteen minutes in the bowels of the earth through a splendidly lighted tunnel, halting suddenly under the sky, and then ascending to the quays of this island. The island, rising in mid-sea, is furnished with solid constructions, spacious quays garnished with the ships of all nations; some bound for the Baltic or the Mediterranean, others arriving from America or India. In the distance to the North, her silver cliffs extending to the North, reflected in the sun, is white Albion, once separated from all the world, now become the British Peninsula. To the South ... is the land of France.... Those white sails spread in the midst of the Straits are the fishing vessels of the two nations.... Those rapid trains which whistle at the bottom of the subterranean station are from London or Paris in three or four hours.

In the spring of 1856, Thomé de Gamond obtained an audience with Napoleon III and expounded his latest plan to him. The Emperor reacted with interest and told the engineer that he would have a scientific commission look into the matter "as far as our present state of science allows." The commission found itself favorable to the idea of the work in general but lacking a good deal of necessary technical information, and it suggested that some sort of preliminary agreement between the British and French Governments on the desirability of the tunnel ought to be reached before a full technical survey was made. Encouraged by the way things seemed to be going, Thomé de Gamond set about promoting his scheme more energetically than ever. He obtained a promise of collaboration from three of Britain's most eminent engineers—Robert Stephenson, Isambard Kingdom Brunel, and Joseph Locke—and in 1858 he traveled to London to advance the cause of the tunnel among prominent people and to promote it in the press. Leading journals were receptive to the idea. An article in the *Illustrated London News* referred to the proposed tunnel as "this great line of junction," and said that it would put an end to the commercial isolation that England was being faced with by the creation on the Continent of a newly unified railway system that was making it possible to ship goods from Central to Western Europe without breaking bulk. The article added that the creation of the tunnel

> ... would still preserve for this country for the future that maritime isolation which formed its strength throughout the past; for the situation of the tunnel beneath the bed of the sea would enable the government on either coast, in case of war, as a means of defense, to inundate it immediately.... According to the calculations of the engineer, the tunnel might be completely filled with water in the course of an hour, and afterwards three days would be required, with the mutual consent of the two Governments, to draw off the water, and reestablish the traffic.

Thomé de Gamond's visit to England was climaxed by a couple of interviews on the subject of the Channel tunnel that he obtained with Prince Albert, who supported the idea with considerable enthusiasm and even took up the matter in private with Queen Victoria. The Queen, who was known to suffer dreadfully from seasickness, told Albert, who relayed the message to Thomé de Gamond, "You may tell the French engineer that if he can accomplish it, I will give him my blessing in my own name and in the name of all the ladies of England." However, in a discussion Thomé de Gamond had earlier had with Her Majesty's Prime Minister, Lord Palmerston, who was present at one of the engineer's interviews with Albert, the idea of the tunnel was not so well received. The engineer found Palmerston "rather close" on the subject. "What! You pretend to ask us to contribute to a work the object of which is to shorten a distance which we find already too short!" Thomé de Gamond quoted him as exclaiming when the tunnel project was mentioned. And, according to an account by the engineer, when Albert, in the presence of both men, spoke favorably of the benefits to England of a passage under the Channel, Lord Palmerston "without losing that perfectly courteous tone which was habitual with him" remarked to the Prince Consort, "You would think quite differently if you had been born on this island."

While Thomé de Gamond was occupied with his submarine-crossing projects, other people were producing their own particular tunnel schemes. Most of them seem to have been for submerged tubes, either laid down directly on the sea bed or raised above its irregularities by vertical columns to form a sort of underwater elevated railway. Perhaps the most ornamental of these various plans was drawn up by a Frenchman named Hector Horeau, in 1851. It called for a prefabricated iron tube containing a railway to be laid across the Channel bed along such judiciously inclined planes as to allow his carriages passage through them without their having to be drawn by smoke-bellowing locomotives—a suffocatingly real problem that most early Channel-tunnel designers, including, apparently, Thomé de Gamond, pretty well ignored. The slope given to Horeau's underground railway was to enable the carriages to glide down under the Channel from one shoreline with such wonderful momentum as to bring them to a point not far from the other, the carriages being towed the rest of the way up by cables attached to steam winches operated from outside the tunnel exit. The tunnel itself would be lighted by gas flames and, in daytime, by thick glass skylights that would admit natural light filtering down through the sea. The line of the tube was to be marked, across the surface of the Channel, by great floating conical structures resembling pennanted pavilions in some medieval tapestry. The pavilions were to be held in place by strong cables anchored to the Channel bottom; they were also to contain marine warning beacons. This project never got under the ground.

In 1858, an attempt to assassinate Napoleon III brought France into the Italian war against Austria, and when word spread in France that the assassin's bombs had been made in Birmingham, a chill developed between the French and British Governments. This led to a wave of fear in England that another Napoleon might try a cross-Channel invasion. All this froze out Thomé de Gamond's tunnel-promoting for several years. He did not try again until 1867, when he exhibited a set of revised plans for his Varne tunnel at the Universal Exhibition in Paris. In doing so he concluded that he had pushed the cause of the tunnel about to the limit of his personal powers. Thirty-five years of work devoted to the problem had cost him a moderate personal fortune, and he was obliged to note in presenting his plan that "the work must now be undertaken by collective minds well versed in the physiology of rocks and the workings of subterranean deposits." After that, Thomé de Gamond retired into the background, squeezed out, it may be, by other tunnel promoters. In 1875, an article in the London *Times* that mentioned his name in passing reported that he was "living in humble circumstances, his daughter supporting him by giving lessons on the piano." He died in the following year.

Although Thomé de Gamond's revised plan of 1867 came to nothing in itself, it did cause renewed talk about a Channel tunnel. The new spirit of free trade was favorable to it among Europeans, and everybody was being greatly impressed with reports of the striking progress on various great European engineering projects of the time that promised closer communication between nations—the successful cutting of the Isthmus of Suez, the near completion of the 8.1-mile-long Mount Cenis rail tunnel, and the opening, only a few years previously, of the 9.3-mile-long St. Gotthard Tunnel, for example. Hardly any great natural physical barriers between neighboring nations seemed beyond the ability of the great nineteenth-century engineers to bridge or breach, and to many people it appeared logical enough that the barrier of the Dover Strait should have its place on the engineers' list of conquests. In this generally propitious atmosphere, an Englishman named William Low took up where Thomé de Gamond left off. Shortly after the Universal Exhibition, Low came up with a Channel tunnel scheme based principally upon his own considerable experience as an engineer in charge of coal mines in Wales. Low proposed the creation of a pair of twin tunnels, each containing a single railway track, and interconnected at intervals by short cross-passages. The idea was a technically striking one, for it aimed at making the tunnels, in effect, self-ventilating by making use of the action of a train entering a tunnel to push air in front of it and draw fresh air in behind itself. According to Low's scheme, this sort of piston action, repeated on a big scale by the constant passage of trains bound in opposite directions in the two tunnels, was supposed to keep air moving along each of the tunnels and between them through the cross-passages in such a way as to allow for its steady replenishment through the length of the tunnels. With modifications, Low's concept of a double self-ventilating tunnel forms the basis for the plan most seriously advanced by the Channel Tunnel Study Group in 1960.

After showing his plans to Thomé de Gamond, who approved of them, Low obtained the collaboration of two other Victorian engineers—Sir John Hawkshaw, who in 1865 and 1866 had had a number of test borings made by a geologist named Hartsink Day in the bed of the Channel in the areas between St. Margaret's Bay, just east of Dover, and Sangatte, just north-east of Calais, and had become convinced that a Channel tunnel was a practical possibility in geological terms; and Sir James Brunlees, an engineer who had helped build the Suez Canal. In 1867, an Anglo-French committee of Channel-tunnel promoters submitted a scheme for a Channel tunnel based on Low's plan to a commission of engineers under Napoleon III, and the promoters asked for an official concession to build the tunnel. The members of the commission were unanimous in regarding the scheme as a workable one, although they balked at an accompanying request of the promoters that the British and French Governments each guarantee interest on a million sterling, which would be raised privately, to help get the project under way, and took no action. But apart from the question of money the promoters were encouraged. In 1870 they persuaded the French Government officially to ask the British Government what support it would be willing to give to the proposed construction of a Channel railway tunnel. Consideration of the question in Whitehall got sidetracked for a while by the outbreak of the Franco-Prussian war in the same year, but in 1872, after further diplomatic enquiries by the French Government, the British Government eventually replied that it found no objection "in principle" to a Channel tunnel, provided it was not asked to put up money or guarantee of any kind in connection with it and provided that ownership of the tunnel would not be a perpetual private monopoly. In the same year, a Channel Tunnel Company was chartered in England, with Lord Richard Grosvenor, chairman of the London, Chatham & Dover Railway, at its head, and with Hawkshaw, Low, and Brunlees as its engineers. The tunnel envisioned by the company would stretch from Dover to Sangatte, and its cost, including thirty-three miles of railway that would connect on the English side with the London, Chatham & Dover and the South-Eastern Railways, and on the French side with the Chemin de Fer du Nord, would be £10,000,000. Three years later, the English company sought and obtained from Parliament temporary powers to buy up private land at St. Margaret's Bay, in Kent, for the purpose of going ahead with experimental tunneling work there. At the same time, a newly formed French Channel Tunnel Company backed by the House of Rothschild and headed by an engineer named Michel Chevalier obtained by act of the French legislature permission from the French Government to start work on a tunnel from the French side at an undetermined point between Boulogne and Calais, and a concession to operate the French section of the tunnel for ninety-nine years. The *cahier des charges* of the French tunnel bill dealt in considerable detail with the terms under which the completed tunnel was to be run, down to providing a full table of tariffs for the under-Channel railroad. Thus, a first-class passenger riding through the tunnel in an enclosed carriage furnished with windows would be charged fifty centimes per kilometre. Freight rates were established for such categories as furniture, silks, wine, oysters, fresh fish, oxen, cows, pigs, goats, and horse-drawn carriages with or without passengers inside.

The greatest uncertainty facing the two companies, now that they had the power to start digging toward each other's working sites, consisted of their lack of foreknowledge of geological obstacles they might encounter in the rock masses lying between the two shores at the neck of the Channel. However, the companies' engineers had substantial reasons for believing that, in general, the region and stratum into which they planned to take the tunnel were peculiarly suited to their purpose. Their belief was based on a rough reconstruction—a far more detailed reconstruction is available nowadays, of course—of various geological events occurring in the area before there ever was a Channel. A hundred million years ago, in the Upper Cretaceous period of the Mesozoic era, a great part of southern England, which had been connected at its easterly end with the Continental land mass, was inundated, along with much of Western Europe, by the ancient Southern Sea. As it lay submerged, this sea-washed land accumulated on its surface, over a period of ten million years, layers of white or whitish mud about nine hundred feet thick and composed principally of the microscopic skeletons of plankton and tiny shells. Eventually the mud converted itself into rock. Then, for another forty million years, at just the point where the neck of the Dover Strait now is, very gentle earth movements raised the level of this rock to form a bar-shaped island some forty miles long. By Eocene times this Wealden Island, stretching westward across the Calais-Dover area, actually seems to have been the only bit of solid ground standing out in a seascape of a Western Europe inundated by the Eocene sea. When most of France and southern England reappeared above the surface, in Miocene times, this island welded them together; later, in the ice age, the Channel isthmus disappeared and emerged again four times with the rise and fall of the sea caused by the alternate thawing and refreezing of the northern icecap. When each sequence of the ice age ended, the land bridge remained, high and dry as ever, and it was over this isthmus that paleolithic man shambled across from the Continent, in the trail of rhinoceroses, hippopotamuses, giant boars, and other great beasts whose fossilized bones have been found in the Wealden area.

Encroaching seas made a channel through the isthmus and cut the Bronze Age descendants of this breed of men off from the Continent about six thousand years ago. Then fierce tidal currents coursing between the North Sea and the Atlantic widened the breach still further until, as recently as four thousand years ago (or only about a couple of thousand years before Caesar's legions invaded Britain by boat), the sea wore away the rock of the isthmus to approximately the present width of the Strait, leaving exposed high at each side the eroded rock walls, formerly the whitish mudbank of Cretaceous times—now the white chalk cliffs of the Dover and Calais areas. Providentially for the later purposes of Channel tunnelers, however, the seas that divided England from the Continent also left behind them a thin remnant of the old land connection in the form of certain chalk layers that still stretched in gentle folds across the bottom of the Strait, and it was through this area of remaining chalk that the Victorian engineers planned to drive their tunnel headings. Even more providentially, they had the opportunity of extending their headings under the Channel through a substratum of chalk almost ideal for tunneling purposes, known as the Lower Chalk. Unlike the two layers of cretaceous rock that lie above it—the white Upper Chalk and the whitish Middle Chalk, both of which are flint-laden, heavily fissured, and water-bearing, and consequently almost impossible to tunnel in for any distance—the Lower Chalk (it is grayish in color) is virtually flint-free and nearly impermeable to water, especially in the lower parts of the stratum, where it is mixed with clay; at the same time it is stable, generally free of fissures, and easy to work. From the coastline between Folkestone and South Foreland, north-east of Dover, where its upper level is visible in the cliffs, the Lower Chalk dips gently down into the Strait in a north-easterly direction and disappears under an outcropping Middle Chalk, and emerges again on the French side between Calais and Cap Blanc-Nez. Given this knowledge and their knowledge of the state of Lower Chalk beds on land areas, the Victorian engineers were confident that the ribbon of Lower Chalk extending under the Strait would turn out to be a continuous one. To put this view to a further test, the French Channel Tunnel Company, in 1875, commissioned a team of eminent geologists and hydrographers to make a more detailed survey of the area than had yet been attempted. In 1875 and 1876 the surveyors made 7,700 soundings and took 3,267 geological samples from the bed of the Strait and concluded from their studies that, except for a couple of localities near each shoreline, which a tunnel could avoid, the Lower Chalk indeed showed every sign of stretching without interruption or fault from shore to shore. However, when these studies were completed, Lord Grosvenor's Channel Tunnel Company did not find itself in a position to do much about them. The company was having trouble raising money, and its temporary power to acquire land at St. Margaret's Bay for experimental workings had lapsed without the promoters ever having used it. William Low, who had left the company in 1873 after disagreements with Hawkshaw on technical matters—Low had come to believe, for one thing, that the terrain around St. Margaret's Bay was unsuitable as a starting place for a channel tunnel—had become the chief engineering consultant of a rival Channel-tunnel outfit that called itself the Anglo-French Submarine Railway Company. But the Anglo-French Submarine Railway Company wasn't getting anywhere, either. It remained for a third English company, headed by a railway magnate named Sir Edward Watkin, to push the Channel-tunnel scheme into its next phase, which turned out to be the most tumultuous one in all its history.

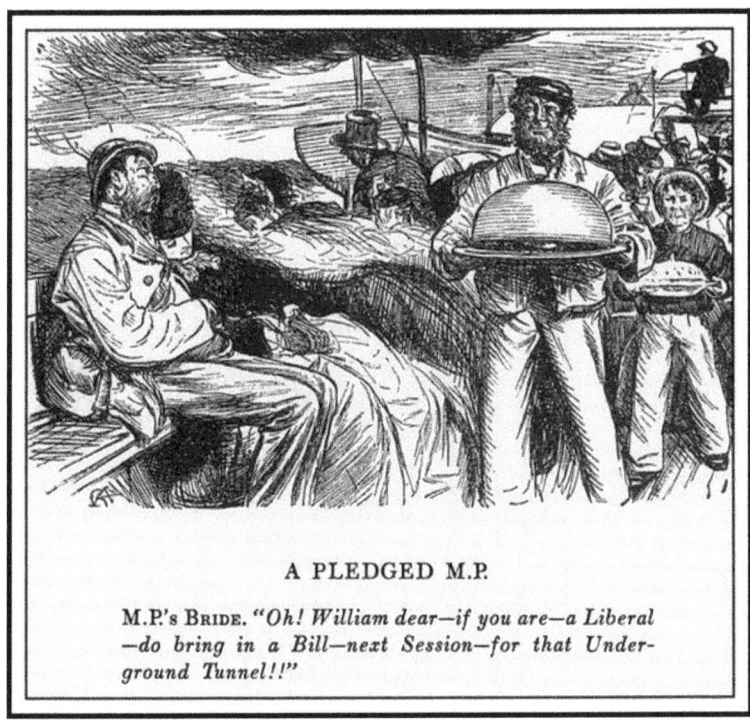

M.P.'S BRIDE. "*Oh! William dear—if you are—a Liberal—do bring in a Bill—next Session—for that Underground Tunnel!!*"

This cartoon depicting the horrors of the Channel crossing originally appeared in *Punch* in 1869. In 1961, 92 years later, *Punch* found it as timely as ever.

THE GREAT TUNNEL SCHEMERS

Aimé Thomé de Gamond

Sir Edward Watkin

THE GREAT ANTI-TUNNELER

Lt.-Gen. Sir Garnet Wolseley, 1882

**Sir Garnet Wolseley's fears of a French invasion through the tunnel
as
seen in the United States in 1882 by *Puck*.**

Hector Horeau's tunnel scheme of 1851 involved laying down a prefabricated submerged tube on the Channel bottom. The pavilions are ventilating stations.

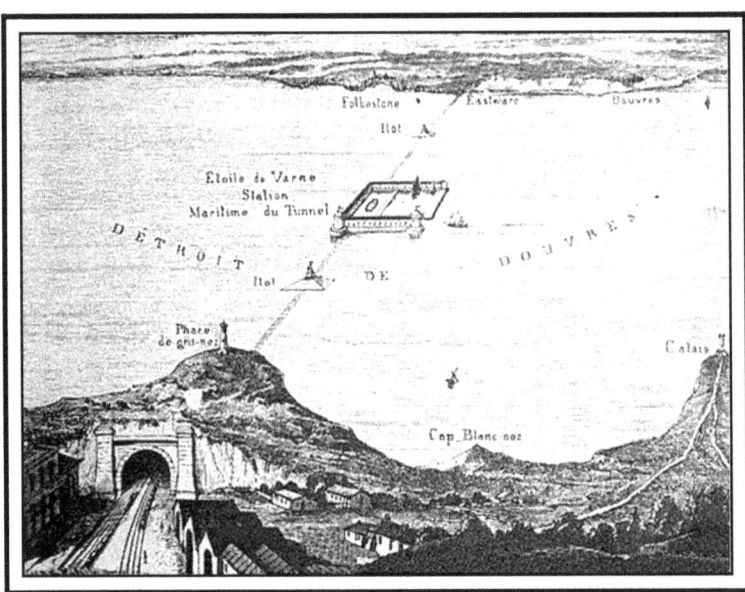

Thomé de Gamond's plan in 1856 for a Channel tunnel by way of the Varne, which would be built up into an international harbor.

The Channel tunnel workings at Shakespeare Cliff in 1882.
The entrance is by the smokestack near the twin portals,
which are unconnected with the tunnel workings.

Diagram of the tunnel workings at Shakespeare Cliff in 1882.
The Admiralty Pier at Dover is in the distance.

TUNNEL PARTIES IN THE 1880s

Everybody who was anybody went down into the tunnel to inspect the new undersea road to France.

1. Guests preparing for the descent.
2. Being lowered 163 feet below the surface to the gallery.
3. Champagne party in the tunnel.

4. Inspecting the Beaumont tunneling machine as it bores toward France.
5. Tunnel oratory at champagne lunch at Dover.

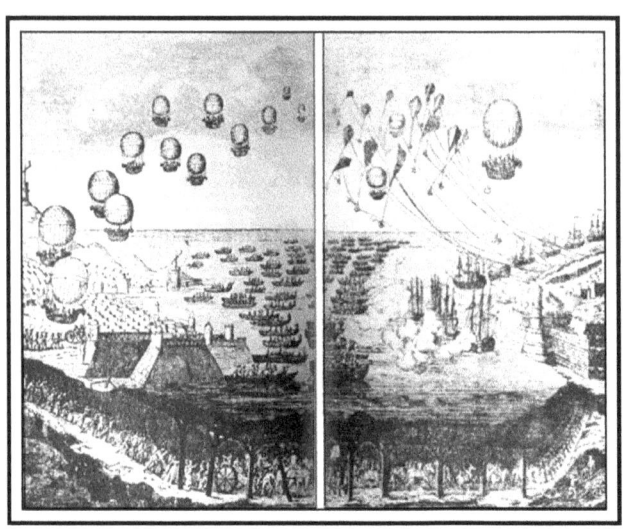

An early Napoleonic vision of the invasion of England
by air, sea, and a Channel tunnel.

Sir Edward Watkin, at the sluice-gates, vanquishes the French invaders
marching on England through the tunnel. A London newspaper cartoon at the time
of the great tunnel controversy.

THREE SOLUTIONS TO THE INVASION PROBLEM

How to have a tunnel and still keep England safe from invasion is a problem that has attracted the attention of artists since the eighties.

**The *Illustrated London News*, 1882, shows how, at the first sign of invasion, the tunnel
could be bombarded from the Admiralty Pier at Dover, from the Dover fortifications,
and from positions offshore.**

Viaduct for the French tunnel entrance proposed in 1906. At signs of French intentions to
invade, the British fleet would sail up and blow this viaduct to smithereens, thus blocking
the tunnel from the French end.

David Langdon in *Paris Match*, 1960, suggests another way of
handling the invasion problem.

PROPOSED METHOD OF CONSTRUCTING A SUBMERGED TUBE
UNDER THE CHANNEL

The illustration shows the proposed laying of a "cut and cover" prefabricated tunnel on the Channel bottom with the aid of a DeLong self-elevating construction platform.

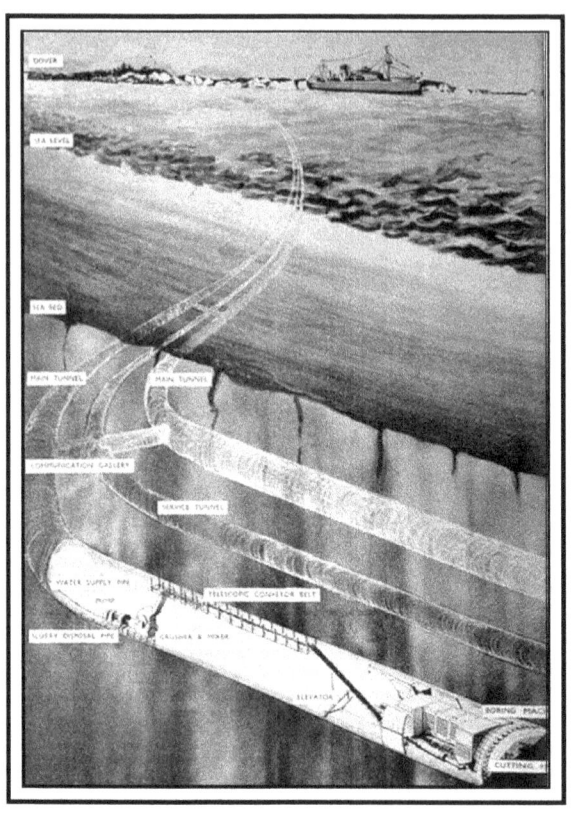

Artist's impression of the boring of the double Channel tunnel, with its extra service tunnel and cross-passages, as proposed by the Channel
Tunnel Study Group in 1960.

Three

SIR EDWARD WATKIN was a vociferously successful promoter from the Midlands. The son of a Manchester cotton merchant, Watkin had passed up a chance at the family business in favor of railways in the early days of the age of steam, and it is a measure of his generally acknowledged shrewdness at railway promotion that in his mid-twenties, having become secretary of the Trent Valley Railway, he negotiated its sale to the London North Western Railway at a profit of £438,000. Now in his early sixties, Watkin was chairman of three British railway companies, the Manchester, Sheffield Lincolnshire Railway, the Metropolitan (London) Railway, and the South-Eastern Railway—the last-named being a company whose line ran from London to Dover via Folkestone—and one of his big current schemes was the formation of a through route under a single management—his own, naturally—from Manchester and the north to Dover. It was while he was busily promoting this scheme that Watkin caught the Channel-tunnel fever. He realized that part of the land the South-Eastern Railway owned along its line between Folkestone and Dover lay happily accessible to the ribbon of Lower Chalk that dipped into the sea in the direction of Dover and stretched under the bed of the Strait, and it wasn't long before he was conjuring up visions of a great system in which his projected Manchester-Dover line, instead of stopping at the Channel shoreline, would carry on under the Strait to the Continent.

One of Sir Edward Watkin's first steps toward determining the technical feasibility of constructing a tunnel was to call in, sometime in the mid-seventies, William Low, whose own tunnel company had quite fallen apart, for engineering consultation. Watkin decided to aim for a twin tunnel based on Low's idea, which would have its starting point in the area west of Dover and east of Folkestone, and he put his own engineers to work on the job. In 1880, the engineers sank a seventy-four-foot shaft by the South-Eastern Railway line at Abbots Cliff, about midway between Folkestone and Dover, and began driving a horizontal pilot gallery seven feet in diameter along the Lower Chalk bed in the direction of the sea off Dover. By the early part of the following year, the experimental heading extended about half a mile underground. His engineers having satisfied themselves that the Lower Chalk was lending itself as well as expected to being tunneled, Sir Edward went ahead and formed the Submarine Continental Railway Company, capitalized at £250,000 and closely controlled by the South-Eastern Railway Company, to take over the existing tunnel workings and to continue them on a larger scale, with the aim of constructing a Channel tunnel connecting with the South-Eastern's coastal rail line. At the same time, he reached an understanding with the French Channel Tunnel Company on co-ordination of English and French operations; he also engineered through Parliament—he was an M.P. himself, and that helped things a bit—a bill giving the South-Eastern power to carry out the compulsory purchase of certain coastal land in the general direction taken by the existing heading.

Then Sir Edward's engineers sank a second shaft, farther to the east but in alignment with the first heading, 160 feet below a level stretch of ground by the South-Eastern Railway line at Shakespeare Cliff, just west of Dover, 120 feet below high water, and began boring a new seven-foot pilot tunnel that dipped down with the Lower Chalk bed leading into the Channel. This second boring, like the first, was carried out with the use of a tunneling machine especially designed for the purpose by Colonel Frederick Beaumont, an engineer who had had a hand in the construction of the Dover fortifications. The Beaumont tunneling machine, a prototype of some of the most powerful tunneling machines in use nowadays, was run by compressed air piped in from the outside, and the discharge of this air from the machine as it worked also served as a way of keeping the gallery ventilated. The cutting of the rock was done by a total of fourteen steel planetary cutters set in two revolving arms at the head of the machine; with each turn of the borer a thin paring of chalk 5/16 of an inch thick was shorn away from the working face, the spoil being passed by conveyor belt to the back of the machine and dumped into carts or skips that were pushed by hand along the length of the gallery on narrow-gauge rails. The machine made one and a half to two revolutions a minute, and Sir Edward estimated for his stockholders that with simultaneous tunneling with the use of similar equipment from the French shore—the French Tunnel Company had already sunk a 280-foot shaft of its own at Sangatte and was preparing to drive a gallery toward England—the Channel bottom would be pierced from shore to shore by a continuous single pilot tunnel, twenty-two miles long, in three and a half years. Once this was done, according to Sir Edward's plans, the seven-foot gallery was to be enlarged by special cutting machinery to a fourteen-foot diameter, and a double tunnel, thickly lined with concrete and connected by cross-passages, constructed. (Four miles of access tunnel were to be added on the French, and possibly on the English, side, too.) The completed tunnel was to be lighted throughout by electric light—a novelty already being tried out in the pilot tunnel by the well-known electrical engineer C. W. Siemens—and the trains that ran through it between France and Britain were to be hauled by locomotives designed by Colonel Beaumont. Instead of being run by smoke-producing coal, the locomotives were to be propelled by compressed air carried behind the engine in tanks, and, like the Beaumont tunneling machine, the engine was supposed to keep the tunnel ventilated by giving out fresh air as it went along. (A lot of air was to be released in the tunnel in the course of a day; a tentative schedule called for one train to traverse it in one direction or another every five minutes or so for twenty hours out of the twenty-four.)

Trains coming through the tunnel from France were to emerge into the daylight and the ordinary open air of England either from a four-mile-long access tunnel connected to the South-Eastern's railway line at Abbots Cliff or—this was a favored alternative plan of Sir Edward's—at Shakespeare Cliff via a station to be constructed in a great square excavated a hundred and sixty feet deep in the ground, which would be covered over with glass, lighted by electric light, and equipped "with large waiting rooms and refreshment rooms." From the abyss of this submerged station, trains arriving from the Continent were to be raised, an entire train at a time, to the level of the existing South-Eastern line by a giant hydraulic lift. (Actually, constructing an elevator capable of raising such an enormous load would not seem as unlikely a feat in the eighties as it might to many people now; Victorian engineers were expert in the use of hydraulic power for ship locks and all sorts of other devices, and, in fact, hydraulic power was so commonly used that the London of half a century ago had perhaps eight hundred miles of hydraulic piping laid below the streets to work industrial presses, motors, and most of the cranes on the Thames docks.)

As the experimental work progressed, Sir Edward Watkin saw to it that all the splendid details about the Channel-tunnel scheme were constantly brought to the attention of the South-Eastern's shareholders, the press, and the public. Sir Edward, besides being a nineteenth-century railway king, was also something of a twentieth-century public-relations operator. He was a firm believer in the beneficial effects of giving big dinners, a pioneer in the art of organizing big junkets, and an adept at getting plenty of newspaper space. An energetic lobbyist in Parliament for all sorts of causes, not excluding his own commercial projects, he was known as a habitual conferrer of friendly little gestures upon important people in and out of government, and his kindness is said to have gone so far at one time that he provided Mr. Gladstone with the convenience of a private railway branch line that went right to the statesman's country home.

The driving of the Channel-tunnel pilot gallery at Shakespeare Cliff offered Sir Edward a handy opportunity for exercising his gifts in the field of public relations, and he took full advantage of it. Week after week, as the boring of the tunnel progressed, he invited large groups of influential people, as many as eighty at a time, including politicians and statesmen, editors, reporters, and artists, members of great families, well-known financiers and businessmen from Britain and abroad, and members of the clergy and the military establishment to be his guests on a trip by special train from London to Dover at Shakespeare Cliff. There, at the Submarine Continental Railway Company workings, the visitors were taken down into the tunnel to inspect the creation of the new experimental highway to the Continent. A typical enough descriptive paragraph in the press concerning one of these visits (on this occasion a group of prominent Frenchmen were the guests of Sir Edward) is contained in a contemporary report in the *Times*:

> The visitors were lowered six at a time in an iron "skip" down the shaft into the tunnel. At the bottom of this shaft, 163 feet below the surface of the ground, the mouth of the tunnel was reached, and the visitors took their seats on small tramcars which were drawn by workmen. So evenly has the boring machine done its work that one seemed to be looking along a great tube with a slightly downward set, and as the glowing electric lamps, placed alternately on either side of the way, showed fainter and fainter in the far distance, the tunnel, for anything one could tell from appearances, might have had its outlet in France.

Sir Edward Watkin, in a speech he made at a Submarine Continental Railway Company stockholders' meeting shortly after such a visit (the main parts of the speech were duly paraphrased in the press), found the effect of the electric light (operated on something called the Swan system) in the tunnel to be just as striking as the *Times* reporter had—only brighter.

> He thought the visit might be regarded as a remarkable one. Their colleague, Dr. Siemens, lighted up the tunnel with the Swan light, and it was certainly a beautiful sight to see a cavern, as it were, under the bottom of the sea made in places as brilliant as daylight.

While on their way by tramcar to view the working of Colonel Beaumont's boring machine at the far end of the tunnel, visitors stopped after a certain distance to enjoy another experience—a champagne party held in a chamber cut in the side of the tunnel. A contemporary artist's sketch in the *Illustrated London News* records the sight of a group of visitors clustered around a bottle-laden table at one of these way side halts. Mustachioed and bearded, and wearing Sherlock Holmes deerstalker caps and dust jackets, they are shown, in tableaued dignity, standing about within a solidly timbered cavelike area with champagne glasses in their hands; and for all the Victorian pipe-trouser formality of their posture there is no doubt that the subjects are having a good time. After such a refreshing pause, the visitors would be helped on the tramcars again and escorted on to see the boring machine cutting through the Lower Chalk and to admire the generally dry appearance of the tunnel, and after that they would be taken back to the surface and given a splendid lunch either in a marquee set up near the entrance to the shaft or at the Lord

Warden Hotel, in Dover, where more champagne would be served, along with other wines and brandies, more toasts to the Queen's health proposed, and speeches made on the present and future marvels of the tunnel, the forwardness of its backers, and the new era in international relations that the whole project promised. These lunches were also convenient occasions for the speakers to pooh-pooh the claims of the rival tunnel scheme of Lord Richard Grosvenor's Channel Tunnel Company, which was still being put forward, although entirely on paper, and to make announcements of miscellaneous items of news about progress in the Lower Chalk.

Thus, at one of these lunches at the Lord Warden Hotel held in the third week of February, 1882, Mr. Myles Fenton, the general manager of the South-Eastern Railway, took occasion to announce to a large party of visitors from London that boring of the gallery had now reached a distance of eleven hundred yards, or nearly two-thirds of a mile, in the direction of the end of the great Admiralty Pier at Dover. According to an account in the *Times*, Mr. Fenton read to the interested gathering a telegram he had received from Sir Edward, who was unable to be present, but who by wire "expressed the hope that by Easter Week a locomotive compressed air engine would be running in the tunnel, of which it was expected the first mile would by that time have been made. (Cheers.)"

Sometimes these lunches were held down in the tunnel itself, and general conditions down there were such that even ladies attended them, on special occasions, as a contemporary magazine account of a visit paid to the gallery by a number of engineers with their families makes clear.

> The visitors were conducted twenty at a time to the end on a sort of trolley or benches on wheels drawn by a couple of men. In the centre of the tunnel a kind of saloon, decorated with flowers and evergreens, was arranged, and, on a large table, glasses and biscuits, etc., were spread for the inevitable luncheon. There was no infiltration of water in any part. In the places where several small fissures and slight oozings had appeared during the boring operations, a shield in sheet iron had been applied against the wall by the engineer, following all the circumference of the gallery and making it completely watertight. There they were as in a drawing-room, and the ladies having descended in all the glories of silks and lace and feathers were astonished to find themselves as immaculate on their return as at the beginning of their trip. The atmosphere in the tunnel was not less pure, but even fresher than outside, thanks to the compressed air machine which, having acted on the

excavator at the beginning of the cutting, released its cooled air in the centre of the tunnel.

With the widespread talk of champagne under the sea, potted plants flourishing under the electric lights, and bracing breezes blowing within the Lower Chalk, going down from London to attend one of Sir Edward's tunnel parties seems to have become one of the fashionable things to do in English society in the early part of 1882. By the beginning of spring, visitors taken down into the tunnel and entertained by Sir Edward included such eminent figures as the Lord Mayor of London, the Archbishop of Canterbury, and the Prince and Princess of Wales. To judge by this stage of affairs, the boring of the tunnel was going on under the most agreeable of auspices.

Behind all the sociability and the stream of publicity engendered in the press by the visits of well-known people to the tunnel, the situation was not quite so promising. While the physical boring was going ahead smoothly enough in the Lower Chalk, the promotion of the tunnel as a full-scale project was encountering growing resistance from within the upper crust of The Establishment. The fact seems to be that the British Government had never felt altogether easy about the idea of the Channel tunnel from the start, and although it had never formally expressed any misgivings about the scheme as a whole, it had always been careful not to associate itself with the enterprise, and its attitude toward its progress generally had been one of reluctant acquiescence. Whatever disquiet people in government felt about the tunnel project appears to have been expressed in three general ways—first, in the introduction of caveats of a military nature; second, in proposals to delay the progress of the scheme on other than military grounds; and third, in a general, nameless suspicion of the whole idea. Such reservations had been evident even in 1875, when the Channel Tunnel Company applied to Parliament for powers to carry out experimental work at St. Margaret's Bay.

To exemplify the first kind of reservation put forward, the Board of Trade, the governmental department under whose surveillance such commercial schemes came, made a point of insisting that for defense purposes the Government must retain absolute power to "erect and maintain such [military] works at the English mouth of the Tunnel as they may deem expedient," and in case of actual or threatened war to close the tunnel down. As for the tendency of governmental people to find other grounds for objection in the project, this could be exemplified by the delaying action of the Secretary to the Treasury, when in 1875 it looked as though Parliament were about to take action on the Channel-tunnel bill. In a memorandum to the Foreign Office, the Secretary sought to have the tunnel bill laid aside at the last moment of its consideration before Parliament so that the answers to all sorts of important jurisdictional questions could be sought—for example, "If a crime were committed in the Tunnel, by what authority would it be cognizable?"[1] And as for the third, unnamed kind of objection, Queen Victoria, who, with her late husband (Prince Albert died in 1861), had once been so enthusiastic about the idea of a Channel tunnel, simply changed her mind about the entire business; in February of 1875, the Queen wrote Disraeli, without elaborating, that "she hopes that the Government will do nothing to encourage the proposed tunnel under the Channel which she thinks very objectionable."

Ever since 1875, all these official doubts and misgivings had continued to lurk in the background of the Government's dealings with the Channel-tunnel promoters—especially military misgivings about the scheme. Apart from putting down the usual bloody insurrections among native populations while she went about the business of maintaining her colonial territories, Britain was at peace with the world. As far as her military relations with the Continent stood, the threats of Napoleon I to invade the island had not been forgotten, and even in the reign of Napoleon III there had been occasional alarms about an invasion, but the country's physical separation from the Continent tended to make the military tensions existing over there seem rather comfortingly remote. Britain's home defenses were left on a pretty easygoing basis, the country's reliance on resistance to armed attack being placed, in traditional fashion, in the power of the Royal Navy to control her seas—meaning, for all practical purposes, its ability to control the Channel. With the Navy and the Channel to protect her shores, Britain in the seventies and eighties got along at home with a professional army of only sixty thousand men, as against a standing army in France of perhaps three-quarters of a million. Seasickness or no seasickness, the Channel was considered to be a convenient manpower and tax-money saver. The advantages of the Channel to Victorian England were perhaps most eloquently expressed by Mr. Gladstone in the course of an article of his in the *Edinburgh Review* in 1870 on England's relationship to the military and political turmoil existing on the Continent. "Happy England!" he wrote in a brief panegyric on the Channel. "Happy ... that the wise dispensation of Providence has cut her off, by that streak of silver sea, which passengers so often and so justly execrate ... partly from the dangers, absolutely from the temptations, which attend upon the local neighborhood of the Continental nations.... Maritime supremacy has become the proud—perhaps the indefectible—inheritance of England." And Mr. Gladstone went on, after dwelling upon one of his favorite themes, the evils of standing armies and the miserable burden of conscription, to suggest that Englishmen didn't realize just how grateful they ought to be for the Channel:

> Where the Almighty grants exceptional and peculiar bounties, He sometimes permits by way of counterpoise an insensibility to their value. Were there but a slight upward

heaving of the crust of the earth between France and Great Britain, and were dry land thus to be substituted for a few leagues of sea, then indeed we should begin to know what we had lost.

These remarks of Mr. Gladstone's on the Channel appear to have made a powerful impression on opinion in upper-class England; for many years after their publication his partly Shakespearean phrase, "the streak of silver sea"—or a variation of it, "the silver streak"—remained as a standard term in the vocabulary of Victorian patriotism. Not surprisingly, considering his views in 1870, the attitude of Mr. Gladstone in 1881 and 1882, during his term as Prime Minister, toward the plan of Sir Edward Watkin to undermine those Straits the statesman had so extolled was an equivocal one.

Indeed, quite a number of people in and around Whitehall had considerably stronger reservations about the Channel-tunnel project than Mr. Gladstone did. These misgivings had to do with fears that a completed tunnel under the Channel might form a breach in England's traditional defense system, and in June of 1881 they first came to public notice in the form of an editorial in the *Times*. Discussing the Channel-tunnel project, the *Times*, while conceding that "As an improvement in locomotion, and as a relief to the tender stomachs of passengers who dread seasickness, the design is excellent," went on to observe that "from a national [and military] point of view it must not the less be received with caution." And the paper asked, "Shall we be as well off and as safe with it as we now are without it? Will it be possible for us so to guard the English end of the passage that it can never fall into any other hands than our own?" The *Times* frankly doubted it, and questioned whether, if the tunnel were built, "a force of some thousands of men secretly concentrated in a [French] Channel port and suddenly landed on the coast of Kent" might not be able by surprise to seize the English end of the tunnel and use it as a bridgehead for a general invasion of England. At the very least, the paper warned, the construction of the tunnel meant that "a design for the invasion of England and a general plan of the campaign will be subjects on which every cadet in a German military school will be invited to display his powers," and it suggested that in the circumstances the Channel had best be left untunneled. "Nature is on our side at present," the *Times* concluded gravely, "and she will continue so if we will only suffer her. The silver streak is our safety." The author of a letter to the *Times* printed in the same issue declared that the tunnel, if constructed, could be seized by the French from within as easily as from without, and that "in three hours a cavalry force might be sent through to seize the approaches at the English end."

To all this Sir Edward Watkin replied easily that the tunnel, when it was finished, could at any time be rendered unusable from the British end by "a pound of dynamite or a keg of gunpowder." However, the negative attitude of a journal as influential as the *Times* was a setback for the project. As a result, the Government increased its caution about the tunnel. When, at the end of 1881, Sir Edward drew up a private bill for presentation during the coming year to Parliament that would formally grant the South-Eastern full authority to buy further coastal lands in the Shakespeare Cliff area and to complete the construction of and to maintain a Channel tunnel (Lord Richard Grosvenor and the proprietors of the London, Chatham & Dover Railway came up with a similar bill on behalf of the Channel Tunnel Company), the Board of Trade held departmental hearings on the rival schemes, and at these hearings further attention was turned to the question of the military security of the tunnel in the event of its being attacked. At these proceedings, Sir Edward, who appeared for the purpose of testifying to the civilizing magnificence of his project, was put somewhat on the defensive by questions about the desirability of the tunnel from a military point of view. He found himself in the disconcerting position of being obliged to show not so much the practicability of building a Channel tunnel as the practicability of disabling or destroying it. However, making the most of the situation, he declared that fortifying the English end of the tunnel, and knocking it out of commission in case of hostile action by another power, was a simple enough matter to be accomplished in any number of ways—by flooding it, by filling it with steam, by bringing it under the gunfire of the Dover fortifications, by exploding electrically operated mines laid in it, or choking it with shingle dumped in from the outside. (There was even mention, at the hearings, of a proposal to pour "boiling petroleum" down upon invaders.) Getting into the spirit of the thing in spite of himself, Sir Edward told the examining committee confidently, "I will give you the choice of blowing up, drowning, scalding, closing up, suffocating and other means of destroying our enemies.... You may touch a button at the Horse Guards and blow the whole thing to pieces."

Notwithstanding Sir Edward's categorical assurances, the wisdom of constructing the tunnel came under vigorous attack at the hearings from a formidably high official military source—from Lieutenant-General Sir Garnet Wolseley, the Adjutant General of the British Army. A veteran of the Crimean War and the Indian Mutiny who was considered to be an expert on the art of surprise attack—his routing of such foes as King Koffee in the first Ashanti War of 1873-74, as well as the great promptitude with which he was said to have "restored the situation" in the Zulu War, made him a well-known figure to the British public—Sir Garnet Wolseley had a dual reputation as an imperialist general and a soldier with advanced ideas on reform of the supply system of the British Army. In fact, his enthusiasm for efficiency was such that the phrase "All Sir Garnet" was commonly used in the Army as a way of saying "all correct." The actor George Grossmith made himself up as Wolseley to sing the part of "a modern Major-General" in performances in the eighties of Gilbert and Sullivan's *The Pirates of Penzance*. Sir Garnet later became Lord Wolseley and Commander-in-Chief of the British Army. Sir Garnet Wolseley's opinions of the tunnel project were very strong ones. In a long memorandum he submitted to the Board of Trade committee examining the tunnel project, he described the Channel as "a great wet ditch" for the protection of England, the like of which, he said, no Continental power, if it possessed one instead of a land frontier, would "cast recklessly away, by allowing it to be tunnelled under." And he denounced the construction of a Channel tunnel on the ground that it would be certain to create what he termed "a constant inducement to the unscrupulous foreigner to make war upon us." In agitated language, General Wolseley invoked the opinion of the late Duke of Wellington that England could be invaded successfully, and he reiterated the fear previously expressed by the *Times* that the English end of the tunnel might be seized from the outside—before any of its defenders had a chance of setting in motion the mechanisms for blocking it up—by a hostile force landing nearby on British soil, whereupon it could readily be converted into a bridgehead for a general invasion of the country. He also declared that "the works at our end of the tunnel may be surprised by men sent through the tunnel itself, without landing a man upon our shores." General Wolseley went on to show just how the deed could be done:

> A couple of thousand armed men might easily come through the tunnel in a train at night, avoiding all suspicion by being dressed as ordinary passengers, and the first thing we should know of it would be by finding the fort at our end of the tunnel, together with its telegraph office, and all the electrical arrangements, wires, batteries, etc., intended for the destruction of the tunnel, in the hands of an enemy. We know that ... trains could be safely sent through the tunnel every five minutes, and do the entire distance from the station at Calais to that at Dover in less than half an hour. Twenty thousand infantry could thus be easily despatched in 20 trains and allowing ... 12 minutes interval between each train, that force could be poured into Dover in four hours.... The invasion of England could not be attempted by 5,000 men, but half that number, ably led by a daring, dashing young commander might, I feel, some dark night, easily make themselves masters of the works at our end of the tunnel, and then England would be at the mercy of the invader.

General Wolseley conceded that an attack from within the tunnel itself would be difficult if even a hundred riflemen at the English end had previously been alerted to the presence of the attackers, but he doubted that the vigilance of the defenders could always maintain itself at the necessary pitch. And he put it to the committee: "Since the day when David secured an entrance by surprise or treachery into Jerusalem through a tunnel under its walls, how often have places similarly fallen? and, I may add, will again similarly fall?" General Wolseley also found highly questionable the efficacy of the various measures proposed for the protection of the tunnel. He declared that "a hundred accidents" could easily render such measures useless. Thus, for example, he found fault with proposals to lay electrically operated mines inside the tunnel ("A galvanic battery is easily put out of order; something may be wrong with it just when it is required ... the gunpowder may be damp"); proposals to admit the sea into the tunnel by explosion ("an uncertain means of defense"); and proposals to flood it by sluice-gates at the English end ("These water conduits [might] become choked or unserviceable when required" and the "drains rendered useless by treachery"). Then, after pointing out all the frailties of the contemplated defenses, General Wolseley went on to assert that the construction of the tunnel would necessitate, at very least, the conversion of Dover at enormous expense into a first-class fortress and that it could very well make necessary the introduction into England on a permanent basis of compulsory military service to meet the increased threat to Britain's national security.

> Surely [Sir Garnet concluded] John Bull will not endanger his birth-right, his property, in fact all that man can hold most dear ... simply in order that men and women may cross to and fro between England and France without running the risk of seasickness.

Sir Garnet reinforced the arguments against the tunnel in personal testimony before the committee. In this testimony he emphasized, among other things, his conviction that once an enemy got a foothold at Dover, England would find herself utterly unable "short of the direct interposition of God Almighty"—an eventuality that Sir Garnet did not appear to count on very heavily—to raise an army capable of resisting the invaders. And the inevitable result of such a default, Sir Garnet told the committee, would be that England "would then cease to exist as a nation."

Sir Garnet's fears for Britain were not shared in a memorandum submitted to the committee by another high Army officer, Lieutenant-General Sir John Adye, the Surveyor-General of the Ordnance. Sir John gave his opinion that "a General in France, having the intention of invading England, would not, in my opinion, count on the tunnel as adding to his resources." He maintained that the argument that the English end of the tunnel might be taken from within could be safely dismissed, as invading troops could be destroyed as they arrived "by means of a small force, with a gun or two, at the mouth of the tunnel." As for the possibility of a hostile force landing on British soil to seize the mouth of the tunnel, he questioned whether "an enemy, having successfully invaded England, [should] turn aside to capture a very doubtful line of communication, when the main object of his efforts was straight before him." General Adye thought that the invaders "would probably feel a much stronger disposition to march straight on London and finish the campaign."

However, the frontal attack on the project by General Wolseley was not a factor to be discounted by any means. Rallying to it in typical fashion, Sir Edward Watkin attempted to stifle the spread of patriotic fears about the tunnel by giving more large lunches at the Lord Warden Hotel at Dover, and he tried to keep all prospects bright by inviting more and more prominent people down into the tunnel at Shakespeare Cliff to marvel at the workings and to refresh themselves with champagne under the electric lights. By mid-February, his guests in the tunnel included no less than sixty Members of Parliament whose support he hoped to obtain for his pending Tunnel Bill, and on one occasion he even succeeded in having the Prime Minister, Mr. Gladstone himself, come down into the tunnel and be shown around. Sir Edward assured his stockholders that what he called "alarmist views" concerning the construction of the tunnel were without any real foundation. Addressing an extraordinary general meeting of the Submarine Continental Railway Company, Sir Edward quoted from an alleged reaction of Count von Moltke on the matter: "The invasion of England through the proposed tunnel I consider impossible. You might as well talk of invading her through that door"—pointing to the entrance to his library. Sir Edward brushed the arguments of military men aside as a collection of "hobgoblin arguments" by "men who would prefer to see England remain an island for ever, forgetting that steam had abolished islands, just as telegraphy had abolished isolated thought." He insisted that the tunnel promoters were engaged in a project at once idealistic and practical, and bravely declared their motto to be identical to that of the South-Eastern Railway Company—"Onwards."

By way of countering Sir Garnet Wolseley's invocation of the opinion of the Duke of Wellington on the dangers of invasion, the promoters put it about that the Duke of Wellington in his day had strongly opposed the construction of a railway between Portsmouth and London on the ground that it would dangerously facilitate the movement of a French army upon London. They asserted that one unnamed but very high English military figure had even expressed alarm, at the time of the Universal Exhibition of 1851, that the English Cabinet did not insist on the Queen's retiring to

Osborne, her country place on the Isle of Wight, because of the large numbers of foreigners at the Exhibition, including three thousand men of the French National Guard, who were allowed to parade the streets of London in uniform, wearing their side arms. And pro-tunnelers recalled in derisive fashion Lord Palmerston's denunciation of the Suez Canal project as "a madcap scheme which would be the ruin of our Indian Empire, were it possible of construction, and which would spell disaster to those who had the temerity to assert it." Colonel Beaumont, as an engineer and military man, too, wrote an article challenging the validity of General Wolseley's conclusions about the tunnel. Colonel Beaumont maintained that Dover might already be regarded as "a first-class fortress, quite safe from any *coup de main* from without." Concerning an attack by bodies of infantry or cavalry through the tunnel, he declared, "They cannot come by train; as, irrespective of any suspicions on the part of the booking clerks, special train arrangements would have to be made to carry [them]; they cannot march, as they would be run over by the trains, running, as they would do, at intervals of ten minutes, or oftener, without cessation, day or night." Colonel Beaumont also outlined, in his article, a number of precautionary measures that could be taken to secure the safety of the English end of the tunnel. They included a system of pumping coal smoke instead of compressed air from a ventilating shaft into the tunnel, and also the provision of a system of iron water mains that would connect the sea with the ventilating shaft and make it possible for the officer of the guard, in case of invasion, to flood the tunnel by turning a stopcock. In accordance with these proposed measures, Sir Edward, early in 1882, attempted to forestall further military criticism of the Channel-tunnel scheme by having such a ventilating shaft sunk at the eastern end of Shakespeare Cliff, about a mile from the main shaft, and having a start made on another horizontal gallery bored from the foot of the new shaft in the direction of the main pilot tunnel under the sea. The new gallery was four feet instead of seven feet in diameter—the smaller aperture in itself being an additional measure of protection, Sir Edward explained, in that intruders would find it impossible to walk along the ventilation shaft in an upright position or in any numbers. A friendly article on the tunnel in the *Illustrated London News* at the beginning of March noted significantly that not only the entrance at the English end—either at Abbots Cliff or at Sir Edward's proposed glassed-in railway station at Shakespeare Cliff—would be under the fire of the eighty-ton turret guns installed on the Admiralty Pier, but that "it is to be observed how completely [the entrance to the new ventilating shaft] is commanded both from the sea and from the Pier, and also from the guns of the fortress." The *Illustrated London News* obligingly showed the principle of the thing by running a large two-page-wide engraving depicting, in handsomely apocalyptic style, the hypothetical destruction of the entire tunnel workings and, presumably, the invaders inside them, amid great ballooning clouds of smoke from gun batteries everywhere—from the end of the Admiralty Pier, from points within the Dover land fortifications, and from the cannonading broadsides of British naval men-of-war standing offshore. The fate of invaders from floodwaters was depicted in a more sensational London publication, the *Penny Illustrated Paper*, which published an engraving a foot and a half long and a foot high illustrating "Sir Edward Watkin's remedy for the invasion scare: Drowning the French Pharaoh in the Channel Tunnel." The engraving showed a cutaway section of the tunnel under the Channel near the English end and, rising upward at the left, a staired chamber of rock equipped with sluice-gates and set in the white cliffs. In this chamber, two figures in top hats and frock coats are standing and gazing down on the tunnel, which is filled with French infantry led by plumed, helmeted officers on horseback. One of the figures in the cliff chamber, evidently meant to represent Sir Edward Watkin, is in the act of calmly operating a turncock that has loosed, through the sluices, a dreadful flood cascading down into the tunnel upon the invaders, who are turning to flee in panic.

Vivid as these scenes of destruction were, they had little effect on the anti-tunnel forces. Already, in February, another attack on the tunnel scheme had appeared in the literary magazine *The Nineteenth Century*, signed by Lord Dunsany. The article, repeating the claim that the tunnel project was a menace to Britain's security, referred to the capacity of the Dover fortress system to defend itself against a modern invading fleet as "contemptible." Lord Dunsany wrote that he had gone down to Dover to examine the famous fortress and had found that with the exception of the two recently installed turret guns on the Admiralty Pier, the guns "generally speaking were of an obsolete pattern—popguns, in fact." And he asserted that when he had remarked on the relatively modern appearance of one of the larger guns in a particularly commanding position of the fortress, "I was told by an artilleryman that there were orders against firing it, as it would bring down the brickwork of the rampart."

Soon after this, an anonymous article in the *Army and Navy Gazette* declared that "The Island has been invaded again and again" and it reminded the *Gazette's* readers that "The present constitution of the country depends on the last successful invasion by a Dutch Prince with Dutch troops, and the overthrow of the King, by an army largely composed of foreigners." The article took Lieutenant-General Sir John Adye severely to task for having found the tunnel a good security risk, and it even went so far afield in its criticism of him as to find fault with the General for what it called his "deliberate, vehement, and long-continued resistance to the introduction of the breech-loading system in our artillery that placed us at the fag-end of all the world, when we ought to have been first."

Then, in March, 1882, *The Nineteenth Century* carried an article against the tunnel by Professor Goldwin Smith, who wrote that the protection of the Channel, by exempting England from the necessity of keeping a large standing army, had preserved the country from military despotism and enabled her to move steadily in the path of political progress. The Channel, Professor Smith wrote, in the past had preserved England from the Armada and from the army of Napoleon I; in the sixteenth and seventeenth centuries it had preserved the Reformation; and in the eighteenth century it had preserved her from the spread of revolutionary fevers and from subjection to foreign tyranny. Now, he said, it was the barrier between Britain's industrial people and military conscription, and he went on, in an echo of Mr. Gladstone's earlier remarks in the *Edinburgh Review*, to declare of the Channel that "A convulsion of nature which should dry it up would be almost as fatal to England as one which should ruin the dykes would be to Holland."

Under these circumstances of increasing controversy, the attitude of the Board of Trade toward the tunnel project became one of further reserve. In February, the Board informed the War Office that the military question of the tunnel had assumed such magnitude that a decision on it should be taken not on a departmental level but on the higher governmental policy level, and it suggested that the War Office start its own investigations on the military aspect of the matter.

Commenting on the prevailing French attitude toward British fears about the tunnel project, the Paris correspondent of the London *Times* observed mildly that "the political uneasiness which the scheme has raised on the other side does not exist here.... No Frenchman, of course, regards it as jeopardizing national security. Frenchmen see in it a greater facility for visiting the United Kingdom, and for relieving the monotony of Swiss tours by a trip to the Scotch highlands."

In satirical fashion, a paragraph in *Punch* undertook to summarize the reaction in another European country:

> Bogie! The Italian Government are so struck by the alarm exhibited by Sir Garnet Wolseley at the prospect of a Channel Tunnel, that they have closed the Mount Cenis and St. Gotthard Tunnels, and left travellers to the mountain diligences. Their reason for doing this is the fact that Napoleon really crossed the Alps, while he only threatened to invade England.

As for reactions in Germany, the British chargé d'affaires in Dresden reported in a dispatch to the Foreign Office that he had questioned the Chief of Staff of the 12th (Saxon) Corps—"an officer of high attainments"—on his attitude toward the possible invasion of England through the Channel tunnel, or through sudden seizure of the English end from the outside.

He wrote that General von Holleben, the officer in question, had observed, in connection with the practicability of landing a Continental force and taking the British end, that although such an operation was not impossible, "that [it] would succeed in the face of our military and moral resources, railways and telegraphs, he should believe when he saw it happen."

> General von Holleben then remarked that the idea of moving an Army-Corps 25 miles beneath the sea was one which he did not quite take in. The distance was a heavy day's march; halts must be made; and the column of troops would be from eight to ten miles long. He was unable to realize all this off hand, and he did not know but what we were talking of a chimoera.
>
> I observed that no one appeared to have asked what would happen to the air of the tunnel if bodies of 20,000 or even 10,000 men were to move through at once. The General said that this atmospheric difficulty was new to him, and it did not sound very soluble.

But the fears of the War Office were not stilled by such observations as these. On February 23, the War Office announced that it was appointing a Channel Tunnel Defense Committee, headed by Major-General Sir Archibald Alison, the chief of British Army Intelligence, to collect and examine in detail scientific evidence on "the practicability of closing effectually a submarine railway tunnel" in case of actual or apprehended war.

The Board of Trade, in the meantime, did its best to hold Sir Edward Watkin and his project off at arm's length. On March 6, 1882, the secretary of the Board of Trade, which had been keeping an eye on newspaper accounts of the progress of the tunnel, wrote to remind Sir Edward of the vital fact that all the foreshore of the United Kingdom below high-water mark at Dover was "*prima facie* the property of the Crown and under the management of the Board of Trade," and that while the department did not wish to impede progress it distinctly wished to give notice that the Government "hold themselves free to use any powers at their disposal in such a matter as Parliament may decide, or as the general interest of the country may seem to them to require." In other words, the Board told the Submarine Continental

Railway Company that it could not drive its tunnel toward France without trespassing on Crown property extending all the way from high-water mark to the three-mile limit of British jurisdiction—the traditionally accepted limit of the carrying power of cannon.

The claim of the Crown to the foreshore in this case was, however, one that Sir Edward Watkin disputed. He claimed that through an arrangement with a landowner near Shakespeare Cliff, and by certain purchases of land from the Archbishop of Canterbury as head of the Church of England, the tunnel proprietors had come into possession of ancient manorial rights, originally granted by the Crown itself, that permitted them to exploit the foreshore at Shakespeare Cliff as they saw fit, including the right to tunnel under it. Sir Edward had claimed that he was having made an extensive legal search of the title in question, which would take a little while.

But the notification from the Board of Trade was an ominous development for Sir Edward and his scheme; and even more ominous signs were to follow. During March, anti-tunneling forces in Britain circulated a great petition among prominent Englishmen against the scheme, for presentation to Parliament. The petition, recording the conviction of the signatories that a Channel tunnel "would involve this country in military dangers and liabilities from which, as an island, it has hitherto been happily free," was published in the April issue of *The Nineteenth Century*, and it was signed not only by military people but by many of the most diversely eminent literary, scientific, and ecclesiastical men of the day—including Robert Browning, Alfred, Lord Tennyson, Herbert Spencer, Professor T. H. Huxley, Cardinals Newman and Manning, and the Archbishop of York—as well as a great cloud of names from the nobility and the landed gentry. In an eloquent article accompanying the petition, the editor of *The Nineteenth Century*, James Knowles, implicitly added the name of William Shakespeare to the list of anti-tunnel signatories by invoking the John of Gaunt speech from *Richard II*:

This royal throne of kings, this scepter'd isle,

This earth of majesty, this seat of Mars,

This other Eden, demi-Paradise,

This fortress built by Nature for herself

Against infection and the hand of war,

This happy breed of men, this little world,

This precious stone set in the silver sea,

Which serves it in the office of a wall

Or as a moat defensive to a house,

Against the envy of less happier lands....

The editor went on to declare, more prosaically, that "To hang the safety of England at some most critical instant upon the correct working of a tap, or of any mechanical contrivance, is quite beyond the faith of this generation of Englishmen."

Almost at the instant that the heavy blow of the petition in *The Nineteenth Century* fell upon the tunnel promoters, the Board of Trade sent down a real thunderbolt upon their heads. On April 1, the Board of Trade wrote Sir Edward Watkin that, whatever might be the title to the foreshore at Shakespeare Cliff, there was no doubt as to the title of the Crown under the bed of the sea below low-water mark and within the three-mile limit. It informed him that according to the department's calculations, based on a tracing of the tunnel route previously obtained from the Submarine Continental Railway Company, the boring of the tunnel now must necessarily be close to the point of low-water mark. And, as a consequence, the Board of Trade instructed the company that, pending the outcome of the Government's deliberations on the military security of the tunnel, it must suspend its boring operations forthwith and give the Government assurances to that effect.

FOOTNOTES.

[1] An Anglo-French Joint Commission formed to set up agreements on the jurisdiction of the two countries over the Channel tunnel in 1876 actually drew up a protocol for a channel-tunnel treaty between England and France. The Commission agreed to the jurisdiction of each government ceasing at a point to be marked in the center of the tunnel and it recommended that the tunnel be regulated by a specially appointed international body.

Four

ALL AT ONCE, it seems, the entire British press was in an uproar of criticism against the Channel tunnel and its unfortunate promoters. The *Sunday Times* pretty well expressed a common reaction of newspapers and periodicals to the latest developments when it said, in an editorial, "We confess to experiencing a feeling of relief on hearing of the interdiction of [Sir Edward Watkin's] progress" in his "working day and night to put an end to that insular position which has in past times more than once proved our sheet anchor of safety. We sincerely hope that Sir E. Watkin's project will shortly receive its final *coup de grâce*. No doubt," it added presciently, "he will not yield without a resolute struggle."

Some hard things were said in the press about the great tunnel promoter. He was accused in various publications of "adroit and unscrupulous lobbying" and of dispensing "profuse hospitality ... persistent and continuous" in pursuit of his scheme. In the May issue of *The Nineteenth Century*, which contained a further number of attacks on the tunnel, Lord Bury reported bitterly on the softening effect that Sir Edward Watkin's public-relations technique had had on a friend of his. Asked if he had signed the great petition against the tunnel, the friend was said to have replied, "No, I have not; I am strongly against the construction of the Tunnel, and I told Watkin so. But he gave a party of us, the other day, an excellent luncheon, and was very civil in showing us everything; so I should not like to do an unhandsome thing to him by signing the protest."

An editorialist in a periodical called *All the Year Round*, which formerly had been put out by Charles Dickens, wrote of the "extraordinary vigor" with which Sir Edward was pushing his tunnel. The editorialist dwelt in satirical fashion on the manner in which prominent persons were "perpetually being whisked down to Dover by special trains, conducted into vaults in the chalk, made amiable with lunch and sparkling wines, and whisked back in return specials to dilate to their friends (and, incidentally, to the public) on the peculiar charm of Pommery and Greno consumed in a chamber excavated far under the sea." The writer found Sir Garnet Wolseley's argument, that the English end of the tunnel could be seized, "on reflection to be perfectly feasible." He asked, "Can anyone suppose that if such a government as that which was formed by the Communists were by any chance ... to rule France, the danger that the temptation to make such a grand coup as the conquest and plunder of England would be too much for them would not be a very real and very present one?" And he wound up by warning "that French troops might checkmate our fleet by simply walking underneath it, and ... take a revenge for Waterloo, the remote possibility of which must make every Englishman shudder."

The probable future effects of the Channel tunnel upon the nervous systems of Englishmen were the subject of intense speculation in most of the press, as a matter of fact. Almost without exception, the prognosis of this hypothetical nervous condition was grave. If, nowadays, the capacity to maintain extraordinary spiritual fortitude under conditions of national emergency has come to be regarded almost as a basic characteristic of the British people, it is a characteristic that the Victorian British press seemed not to be aware of. Almost unanimously, the press warned that part of the price of constructing a tunnel would be the occurrence of wild periodic alarms among the population. "Perpetual panics and increased military expenditure are the natural result of such a change as that which will convert us from an island into a peninsula," an editorial in *John Bull* declared. The London *Daily News* demanded to know whether "anyone who is in the least acquainted with English character and history" could deny the country's susceptibility to periodic panics. The *Daily News* dwelt apprehensively on the inevitable result of panics arising out of the construction of a Channel tunnel:

> We should be constantly beginning expensive and elaborate schemes for strengthening the defences according to the fashionable idea of the day.... They would be about half carried out by the time the next panic occurred, and then they would be obsolete.... Now it would be elaborate fortifications at Dover itself; now a great chain of forts to hem it in from inland; now the old scheme of the fortification of London; now the establishment of forts out at sea over the tunnel.... Is it worth while to run the chance...?

The most diverse arguments were advanced in the press against the construction of the tunnel. In the May issue of *The Nineteenth Century*, Major-General Sir E. Hamley raised the question of whether the French, invading Britain by train through the tunnel, might not seize some distinguished English people and carry the captives along on the engine as hostages, so that however thoroughly the officer in charge of the defensive apparatus at the English end were alerted to their presence, "still he might well be expected to pause if suddenly certified that he would be destroying, along with the enemy in the Tunnel, some highly important Englishmen." Another writer, referring to the responsibility and possibly also to the character of the officer in charge of the tunnel defenses, observed thoughtfully that "the commandant of Dover would carry the key of England in his pocket." Still another commentator wondered if responsibility for making a decision to blow up the tunnel might not be too much even for an English Prime Minister:

> The Premier might think himself justified in destroying twenty millions of property ... but also, he might not. He might be an undecided man, or a man expecting defeat by the Opposition, or a man paralyzed by the knowledge that the tunnel was full of innocent people whom his order would condemn to instant death, in a form which is at once most painful and most appalling to the imagination. They would all be drowned in darkness. The responsibility would be overwhelming for an individual, and a Cabinet, if dispersed, takes hours to bring together.

In his article in *The Nineteenth Century* Lord Bury, going under the assumption that a Prime Minister in a period of gravest national emergency would indeed be able to haul his Cabinet colleagues and military advisers together in reasonable time to consider having the tunnel blown up, asked his readers to conjure up the painful scene at Downing Street:

> Imagine him for a moment sitting in consultation. His military advisers tell him that the decisive moment has come. "I think, gentlemen," says the minister, turning to his colleagues, "that we are all agreed—the Tunnel must be immediately destroyed. Fire the mine!" "There is one other point," says the officer, "on which I request instructions—at what time am I to execute the order?" "At once, sir; telegraph at once, and in five minutes the blasting charge can be fired." "But," persists the officer, "trains laden with non-combatants are at this moment in the Tunnel. They enter continuously at twenty minutes' intervals; there are never less than four trains, two each way, in the Tunnel at the same time; each train contains some three hundred persons ... I could not destroy twelve hundred non-combatants without very special instructions."

And Lord Bury asked, "What would any minister, under such circumstances, do?"

As for the proposed defensive measure of flooding the tunnel in case of invasion, General Sir Lintorn Simmons, writing in the same issue of *The Nineteenth Century*, considered it to be a dubious one at best, since, he observed, "it is not to be believed that a great country like France, with the engineering talent she possesses, could not find the means" of pumping all the flood waters out again.

An assertion by Dr. Siemens, the electric-lighting expert, that the tunnel could easily be rendered unusable to invaders if its British defenders would pump carbonic-acid gas into it to asphyxiate the intruders, was similarly challenged, in the correspondence columns of the *Times*, by a scientific colleague of his, Dr. John Tyndall. Dr. Tyndall offered to wager Dr. Siemens that the latter could in six hours devise countermeasures that would enable troops to pass unscathed through the tunnel, gas or no gas. Dr. Tyndall illustrated his point by describing an experiment he said he had made on the very day of his letter, while coming down home from London by train, on a part of the South-Eastern line where the speed was thirty miles an hour:

> I took out my watch and determined how long I could hold my breath without inhalation. By emptying my lungs very thoroughly, and then charging them very fully, I brought the time up to nearly a minute and a half. In this interval I might have been urged through more than half a mile of carbonic-acid gas with no injury and with little inconvenience to myself.

Dr. Tyndall concluded, firmly, "The problem of supplying fresh air to persons surrounded by an irrespirable atmosphere has been already solved by Mr. Fleuss and others."

Then there were even more disturbing objections. Could the defenders at the English end always be relied on as absolutely loyal Englishmen? *The Field*, without naming any names, wrote of "proof that in the United Kingdom itself ... there are numbers of daring and reckless persons" who, "to gain their sinister ends ... would not hesitate to sacrifice the independence of the country." Frankly, the paper feared possible acts of treachery in the tunnel by "a handful of unprincipled desperadoes." And the *Spectator*, visualizing the thing in more detail, suggested that its readers "consider ... the danger of treachery ... the rush on the tunnel being made by Irish Republicans in league with the French, while the wires of the telegraph were cut, and all swift communications between Dover and London suddenly suspended." Taking all the risks of the tunnel into account, the *Spectator* said it could not bring itself to believe that "even in this age, with its mania for rapid riding and comfortable locomotion, such a project will be tolerated." The *Sunday Times*, for its part, pointed out that, as things stood, "the silver streak is a greater bar to the movements of Nihilists [and] Internationalists ... than is generally believed." But, it added, "with several trains a day between Paris and London, we should have an amount of fraternising between the discontented denizens of the great cities of both countries, which would yield very unsatisfactory results on this side of the Channel."

Meetings and debates to discuss the tunnel menace were held all over England, and even at a meeting of so progressive an organization as the Balloon Society of Great Britain, which was held in the lecture room of the Royal Aquarium at Westminster, the subject was discussed with "some warmth of feeling ... on both sides." There was a wide circulation of sensational pamphlets, written in pseudohistorical style, that purported to chronicle the sudden downfall of England at the end of the nineteenth century through the existence of a Channel tunnel—Dover taken, the garrison butchered, the English end of the tunnel incessantly vomiting forth armed men, London invaded, and England enslaved—all of this in a few hours' time.

In contrast to these manifold cries of alarm among the English, it seems never to have occurred to anybody in France at the time seriously to suggest that if a tunnel were to be constructed, a hostile English force, supported by an English navy in control of the Channel sea, might suddenly seize the French entrance by surprise and use it as a bridgehead for a general invasion of France. A few French commentators did, however, remind the anti-tunnel forces in England that while the English had set hostile foot on French soil some two or three times in as many centuries—not to mention her having kept physical control over the port of Calais for over two hundred years following the Battle of Crécy—English soil had remained untouched by France. Most of the French newspapers appeared to be unable to fathom the cause of the whole tunnel commotion, which was generally put down to English eccentricity. Several French journals, surveying all the fulminations on the other side of the Channel, even took an attitude toward the English of a certain detached sympathy. One of the more interesting French commentaries on the uproar in England appeared in the *Revue des Deux Mondes*. In this article, the author expressed some doubt that British military men who denounced the dangers of the tunnel were really convinced of the reality of those dangers. For them to do so, he suggested, one would have to presuppose, on one side of the Channel, a "France again a conqueror with, at her head, a man gifted with ... an incredible depth in crime; a secret, an almost incredible diligence in preparation as in execution," and, on the other side, "a governor of Dover who would be an idiot or a traitor, a War Minister who would not possess the brain of a bird, a Foreign Minister who would allow himself to be deceived in doltish fashion." How could the French possibly assemble perhaps a thousand railway carriages in England without arousing the suspicions of British Intelligence? How could the vanguard of the French invaders get through the tunnel with all their required ammunition, horses, and supplies, and get them all unloaded in a few minutes—would this vanguard sally forth without biscuits? The author found no solution to these particular problems. Instead, he devoted himself to the larger issue:

> The day the inauguration of the Submarine Tunnel will be celebrated, England will no longer be an island, and that is a stupendous event in the history of an island people.... Islanders have always considered themselves the favorites of Providence, which has undertaken to provide for their security and independence.... They congratulate themselves on their separation from the rest of the world by natural frontiers over which nobody can squabble. They feel that they hold their destiny in their own hands, and that the effect of the follies and crimes of others could not reach them.... Their character is affected by this. Like Great Britain, every Englishman is an island where it is not easy to land.

And the article asked, wonderingly, "What would an England that was not an island be?"

The deliberations of the scientific investigating committee appointed by the War Office and presided over by Sir Archibald Alison lasted from the latter part of February until the middle of May. In the committee's report of its findings to the War Office, the complexity and solemn nature of the questions laid before it were indicated by their mere classification and subclassification. Thus, the contingencies for rendering a Channel tunnel absolutely useless to an enemy were considered under the headings of:

I. Surprise from Within
II. Attack from Without

And the committee reported that it had considered measures to secure the tunnel against (I) under such subcategories as:

1. Fortifications
2. Closure or temporary obstructions
3. Explosion by mines or charges
4. Flooding
a. Temporary
b. Permanent

After reviewing the situation in great detail, and from every aspect, the committee suggested a long list of precautionary measures that, it said, it would be necessary to use, singly or in combination, to protect and seal off the tunnel against any enemy attempts to invade England directly through the tunnel or by seizing the English end from the outside and using it as a bridgehead for invasion. The list included these recommendations:

The mouth of the tunnel should be protected by "a portcullis or other defensible barrier."

A trap bridge should be set in connection with this portcullis.

Means should be provided for closing off the ventilation, and for "discharging irrespirable gases or vapors into the tunnel."

Arrangements should be made for rapidly discharging loads of shingle into the land portion of the tunnel, shutting it off.

The land portion of the tunnel should be thoroughly mined with explosives capable of being fired by remote control exercised not only from within the central fort at Dover but also from more distant points inland, so that even if the protective fortress fell to the enemy, the tunnel still could be permanently destroyed.

In addition, a truck loaded with explosives and equipped with a time fuse should be kept ready by the entrance, so that it could be sent coasting down into the tunnel for some distance, there to explode automatically.

Arrangements should be made for temporarily flooding the tunnel by means of culverts operated by sluice valves. ("If by chance the sluice valves should not act, Measure XVIII could be resorted to, or the tunnel could be blocked by one or more of the means ... mentioned in Measures VIII, IX, X, XI, and XII.")

The tunnel should emerge inland, out of firing range from the sea. And it was imperative that it emerge under the guns and "in the immediate vicinity of a first-class fortress, in the modern acceptation of the term, a fortress which could only be reduced after a protracted siege both by land and sea."

And so on.

Even after drawing up all these elaborate precautions for closing the tunnel from the English end, the Channel Tunnel Defense Committee was left with some nagging doubts about their adequacy. In a concluding paragraph of its report, the committee pointed out that "it must always be borne in mind that, in dealing with physical agencies, an amount of uncertainty exists," and that it was "impossible to eliminate human fallibility." As a consequence, the members stated cautiously, "it would be presumptuous to place absolute reliance upon even the most comprehensive and complete arrangements."

The committee also agreed, almost as an afterthought, that the Channel tunnel proposed by Sir Edward Watkin could not be sanctioned in the form envisaged, on the grounds that it did not meet the committee's conditions for emerging inland, out of firing range from the sea, and in the immediate vicinity of a first-class fortress. It also rejected, on the first of these grounds, a proposal by the lesser Channel Tunnel Company for a tunnel that would start from within Dover and for the sake of easy destructibility run right under a nearby corner of Dover Castle—and on the grounds that this entrance would be *too* much in the vicinity of a fortress. And the committee objected that since the proposed entrance would emerge "in the heart of the main defences and in the midst of the town" any fire from these defenses "would inflict great injury on the town and its inhabitants, and the general defence would be much embarrassed."

At the War Office, the report of the Alison committee was supplemented by another long memorandum on the tunnel question by Sir Garnet Wolseley. In this document of some twenty thousand words, which was conveniently furnished with numerous marginal headings like "Why tunnels through the Alps afford no argument in favor of the Channel Tunnel," "The Tunnel an acknowledged danger," "What national advantage then justifies its construction," "Many tunnels will be constructed," "What we owe to the Channel," and "Danger of surprise of our fortifications without warning! Fatal result!!," Sir Garnet recapitulated and elaborated at great length upon his previous arguments against the tunnel and added several new ones. Sir Garnet went into fine detail concerning the possibility of a sudden seizure of the English end of the tunnel and, simultaneously, Dover, by the French. For example, to his previous description of how hostile French forces might come by train through the tunnel dressed in ordinary clothes he added the detail that they might also travel in the carriages "at express speed, with the blinds down, in their uniforms and fully armed"—their co-conspirators at the other end meanwhile having rendered it "not likely that ticket-takers or telegraph operators on the French side would be allowed any channel of communicating with us until the operation had been effected." Sir Garnet was equally explicit about the situation at Dover. Warning that "the civilian may start in horror at the statement that Dover could also be taken by surprise," General Wolseley declared that, as things stood, anybody at all, any night, was free to walk up to any of the forts at Dover, and, "if he would announce himself to be an officer returning home to barracks, the wicket would be opened to him, and if he entered he would see but two men, one the sentry, the other the noncommissioned officer who had been roused up from sleep by the sentry to unlock the gate." General Wolseley demonstrated how such a caller might well be "a dashing partisan leader" of a French raiding party that had landed in Dover in the dead of night, in calm or foggy weather, from steamers, and had already quietly knocked down and silenced any watchman or other witnesses in the dark area. He showed how such a *soi-disant* English officer and his accomplices "might thus easily obtain an entrance into every fort in Dover; the sentry and the sleepy sergeant might be easily disposed of. The rifles of our sentries at home are not loaded, and the few men on guard [could be] made prisoners whilst asleep on their guard bed." Thus, General Wolseley said, the intruders could quickly effect the seizure of all the forts in Dover—"In an hour's time from the moment when our end of the tunnel was taken possession of by the enemy, large reinforcements could reach Dover through the tunnel, and ... before morning dawned, Dover might easily be in possession of 20,000 of the enemy, and every succeeding hour would add to that number." With Dover done in, London would be next, and the future commander-in-chief of the British Army went on to show how the enemy force, now swelled to 150,000 men, once it reached London and occupied the Thames from there to the arsenal at Woolwich, could dictate its own terms of peace, which he estimated at a rough guess as the payment of six hundred million pounds and the surrender of the British Fleet, with the English end of the tunnel remaining permanently in the hands of the French, so that "the perpetual yoke of servitude would be ours for ever."

Concerning all the various measures proposed to protect the tunnel, Sir Garnet had no confidence in them at all. He stressed once more the unreliability of anything mechanical or electrical, and he added the new argument that whatever secret devices, such as mines, were installed in the tunnel for its protection were bound to come to the knowledge of the enemy sooner or later. Any military secret, General Wolseley said, was a purchasable secret; he illustrated his argument with an observation concerning a meeting between Napoleon I and Alexander I of Russia:

> No two men were more loyally followed or had more absolute authority than Napoleon and Alexander. No two men had a stronger wish or stronger motive for keeping secret the words which passed between them personally in a most private conference in a raft in the middle of a river. Yet, by paying a large sum our Ministry obtained the exact terms of the secret agreement the two had there arrived at. Moreover, our Ministry obtained that information so immediately that they were able to act in anticipation of the designs formed by the two Emperors.

Finally, having discussed, in the most elaborate fashion, all the measures that his previous opposition to the scheme had caused to be proposed for the defense of the tunnel, Sir Garnet condemned them on the ground of their very elaborateness. "If in any one of these respects our security fails, it fails in all," he wrote of the multiple precautions recommended by Sir Archibald Alison's scientific committee. Thus, in General Wolseley's eyes, the defense of the tunnel was foredoomed as a self-defeating process, and was therefore a practical impossibility.

The question of the multiplicity of the proposed defenses was handled in different fashion in a further War Office memorandum on the tunnel, issued by the Duke of Cambridge, the Army Commander-in-Chief and a cousin of Queen Victoria. "Nothing has impressed me more with the magnitude of the danger which the construction of this proposed tunnel would bring with it," the Duke of Cambridge wrote, "than the amount of precautions and their elaborateness [proposed by] this Scientific Committee.... If this danger was small, as some would have the country believe, why should all these complicated precautions be necessary?" The Duke of Cambridge fully endorsed the position taken by Sir Garnet Wolseley. He protested "most emphatically" against the construction of a Channel tunnel and "would most earnestly beg Her Majesty's Government" to consider with the utmost gravity the perils of surprise attack upon the country arising out of even a modified scheme that would take into account the recommendations of the Alison committee.

To his memorandum His Royal Highness appended a copy of a report that he had had his intelligence service put together specially in connection with the tunnel question—a long account purporting to show some hundred and seven instances occurring in the history of the previous two hundred years where hostilities between states had been started without any prior declaration of war, or even any decent notification.

If anything seemed likely to have been successfully blocked up and finished off under all this bombardment, it was Sir Edward Watkin's Channel-tunnel scheme. Curiously enough, the Board of Trade, which had ordered the tunnel workings stopped back in April and had no intention of issuing a working permit for them now, was not altogether convinced of this. In fact, since April the Board had been developing the suspicion that something peculiar might be going on down under the sea at Shakespeare Cliff. Back in the early part of April, the Board of Trade's order to the Submarine Continental Railway Company to stop its tunneling activities was received, as one might expect, with some anguish. The first formal reaction was a letter from the permanent secretary of the company to T. H. Farrer, the secretary of the Board of Trade, saying that the company would of course acquiesce in the orders of the board, but begging, at the same time, to be allowed to continue the present gallery extending from the main, or Number Two, shaft at Shakespeare Cliff a short distance further, so as to be able to complete the first stage of the works—the junction of the main gallery with the new gallery extending from the ventilating, or Number Three, shaft. This letter was followed on April 9 by another from Sir Edward Watkin addressed to Joseph Chamberlain, the president of the Board of Trade, urgently repeating the request, this time on the ground of safety. Sir Edward wrote Mr. Chamberlain:

> The moment the Board of the Tunnel Company decided to obey you, I peremptorily ordered the works to be stopped. The [boring] machine has been silent since Thursday

evening. But the Engineer sends me a very startling report and warning.

> He fears *defective ventilation* [owing to stoppage of the air-driven boring machine] and danger to life—quite apart from depriving a fine body of skilled workmen of their bread, and general loss and damage in money. I can only reply to him that I am acting under your order. Still ... this is the first time the ventilation of a mine has been so interfered with. Should the engineer's alarm be well founded, and should men faint from bad air at the end of the gallery, there would be no means of getting them out alive.

Sir Edward added, without changing his tone of humane agitation, that only the day before he had received a request from the Duke of Edinburgh to be allowed to see the tunnel workings, along with the Duchess, ten days hence, and that the Speaker of the House of Commons had already arranged to visit the tunnel "on Saturday, the 22nd, leaving Charing Cross at eleven." "What must be done?" he asked. Mr. Chamberlain replied promptly by telegraph that if the stopping of the machinery in the tunnel was constituting a danger to life, he authorized Sir Edward, pending further investigation of the situation by the Board of Trade, temporarily to keep the machinery going to the extent of preventing this danger. However, he followed up this telegram with a letter to Sir Edward in which he expressed himself as being "not able to understand the exact nature of the physical danger anticipated" by Sir Edward in the tunnel if the workings were stopped. "I do not see the necessity for workmen remaining in the tunnel where the ventilation is likely to be defective," Mr. Chamberlain observed. He added that he was making arrangements to have one of the Board of Trade inspectors visit the tunnel to investigate the situation.

On April 11, the Board of Trade duly telegraphed Sir Edward that its chief inspector of railways, Colonel Yolland, of the Royal Engineers, would be at Dover at noon the next day to investigate the ventilation problem in the tunnel. Sir Edward, however, wired back that he was unable to meet the Colonel at Dover that day and could not make an appointment with him "until after the visit to the works of the Duke of Edinburgh on Tuesday next."

To this the Board of Trade replied, on April 13, that Colonel Yolland had been instructed to visit the tunnel works "entirely out of regard to the very urgent and grave question raised in your letter ... respecting the ventilation of the boring" and that the department was finding it difficult to understand why Colonel Yolland's visit to the tunnel should be postponed. Sir Edward's answer to this was to invite Mr. Chamberlain down into the tunnel personally, so that Sir Edward could "show and explain everything," since "until you have seen, and had explained to you, on the spot as Mr. Gladstone did and had, and as we hope the Duke of Edinburgh will next Tuesday, the nature and condition of our works, it is, in my humble judgement, impossible to discuss the question with exactitude." He said nothing about the possibility of Mr. Chamberlain's or the Duke and Duchess of Edinburgh's being asphyxiated in the tunnel. Mr. Chamberlain declined the invitation; he said he had ordered Colonel Yolland down to Dover immediately to report on the tunnel. But Colonel Yolland didn't get down into the tunnel to make an inspection that month. Some impediment, some unanticipated difficulty always seemed to arise when things appeared to be about to straighten themselves out. By the beginning of May, the Board of Trade, still trying, flatly informed Sir Edward that Colonel Yolland and Walter Murton, its solicitor, would inspect the tunnel workings on May 6. But on May 4 the general manager of the South-Eastern Railway replied that "Sir Edward Watkin wishes me to say that he regrets very much that it will be quite impossible to arrange for such inspection to take place on that date." He suggested that Sir Edward could arrange it for the 13th. The Board of Trade, replying immediately, insisted on its taking place "not later than Wednesday next." That letter was met with the answer that "Sir Edward Watkin is at present out of town, and is not expected to return until early next week." He must have stayed out of town quite a while, because the Board of Trade heard nothing from the company until May 18, when the directors of the company, writing jointly, told the department that while they acquiesced in the request of Colonel Yolland and Mr. Murton to visit the tunnel, unfortunately "the machinery is under repair," and as a consequence "it would not be ... safe for those gentlemen to go down the shaft." However, the directors added, hopefully, they felt sure that "by working the machinery, air compressors, and pumping engines for a few days and nights" their engineers could get everything in order for a proper tour of inspection. On May 24 Mr. Murton tried again. He wrote the tunnel proprietors, notifying them that "Colonel Yolland and myself propose to inspect the tunnel works on Saturday next the 27th instant." But the company's reply to the letter was regretful. It said that "the repairs to the winding engine cannot be completed until after Whitsuntide."

Meanwhile, Mr. Murton was having his difficulties with the solicitor of the South-Eastern over the legal question of the company's claims to ancient manorial rights to the use of the foreshore at Shakespeare Cliff, as the tone of various letters he was obliged to write indicates. For example:

> DEAR SIR,
>
> May I remind you that I have not yet received the abstract of title; I beg that you will at once send it to me....
>
> > "I am, & c.,
> > WALTER MURTON."

Or again:

> DEAR SIR,
>
> I am without answer to my letter of the 31st ultimo. I beg you will let me know without further delay whether you do or do not propose to send me abstract of title.
>
> > "I am, & c.,
> > WALTER MURTON."

Or yet again:

> DEAR SIR,
>
> Will you kindly write me a reply to my letters which I can send on to the Board of Trade.
>
> > "Yours, & c.,
> > WALTER MURTON."

By June 9, the Board of Trade became quite out of patience over the matter of inspecting the tunnel. Introducing an ominous note, it informed Sir Edward that Mr. Chamberlain "feels that he must insist upon this visit of inspection, and if he understands that permission is refused, will be compelled to place the matter in the hands of his legal advisers, with the view of determining and enforcing the rights of the Crown." Sir Edward was indignant. In reply, he declared that he was being subjected to an "undeserved threat." Mr. Chamberlain, responding, denied that the threat was undeserved. He wrote firmly:

> Hitherto, on one ground or another, this inspection has been again and again postponed.

> I am bound to guard the rights of the Crown in this matter, and I desire to ascertain whether those rights have up to the present time been in any way invaded.
>
> This is the object of the inspection, and as it will not brook delay ... I have only now to ask an immediate answer stating definitely when it can take place.

Sir Edward's answer was once more to beg Mr. Chamberlain himself to join a party of prominent visitors going down to see the tunnel; he added that "Colonel Yolland shall be at once communicated with."

But by various intervening circumstances—joint letters got up by the tunnel promoters to the Prime Minister and to the Board of Trade protesting hard treatment, and so on—the Board of Trade found itself brooking delays all through the month of June. On June 26, the Board of Trade wrote in stern fashion to Sir Edward that the demands of the Board of Trade to inspect the tunnel workings "have been repeatedly formulated and persistently evaded on behalf of the Submarine Continental Railway Company," and that the only way the company could avoid legal action by the Crown was "to consent *at once* to the proposed inspection." There was no satisfactory reply from the tunnel proprietors, and on July 5 the Board of Trade, after due notification to the Submarine Continental Railway Company, obtained an order from Mr. Justice Kay, in the High Court of Justice, restraining the tunnel promoters and their employees from "further working or excavating, or taking or interfering with any chalk, soil, or other substance" in the Channel tunnel without the consent of the Board of Trade, and ordering them to give the department access to the tunnel to inspect the workings. In the course of these judicial proceedings, a number of affidavits presented to Mr. Justice Kay by the Government revealed the interesting information that the Board of Trade, finding itself unable to obtain access for its inspectors into the tunnel, for some time past had felt itself obliged to station watchers on top of Shakespeare Cliff and on the sea regularly to spy upon the tunnel workings and to count the number of bucketfuls of soil it maintained had been removed from the workings. And, according to all its calculations, the Board of Trade had little doubt that the proprietors of the Submarine Continental Railway Company were deliberately and surreptitiously tunneling under the sea below low-water mark, on Crown property, and burrowing into and removing chalk of the realm.

Intimation of what was in store for him in the High Court of Justice reached Sir Edward Watkin at the very time that he was showing a party of distinguished people, including Ferdinand de Lesseps, the builder of the Suez Canal, around the tunnel. A glimpse of that interesting visit is contained in a report in the London *Times*:

> M. de Lesseps, while down in the tunnel and under the sea, proposed the health of the Queen, remarking that the completion of the work was required in the interest of mankind.
>
> When all the visitors were again above ground, luncheon was served in a marquee.
>
> Sir E. Watkin, in proposing the health of M. de Lesseps, remarked that there were those in our country who seemed to consider that the work of the company they had just inspected was a crime. He had just received a telegram informing him that he would have to answer on Wednesday next at the instigation of the President of the Board of Trade before a court of law for having committed the crime of carrying on these experiments. (Hisses and groans.)

Somewhat revealingly, Sir Edward added, when the signs of indignation subsided, that

> For his own part, if he was to be committed by a court of law for contempt, he should have this consolation—that the proceedings which had been taken against him had been delayed sufficiently long to enable him with his colleagues to have the honor of entertaining M. de Lesseps, in whom he should have a witness, if he had to call one, to prove that they had been engaged in a work which had been as successful as he believed it would be ultimately useful.

At long last, supported by all the might of the Crown, Colonel Yolland got to the tunnel on July 8 to make his inspection of the workings. But upon his arrival there he found, to his chagrin, that "I was not provided, at the time ... with all the necessary means for making the measurements, and taking the requisite bearings" in the tunnel, and he was obliged to put his inspection off once more. Properly equipped, he descended into the tunnel a week later, on Saturday, July 15, and inspected everything, including the boring apparatus that Sir Edward had insisted had to be used to ventilate the gallery and prevent loss of life. What Colonel Yolland found there caused the Board of Trade, five days later, to send a most severe letter to the tunnel proprietors. In it, the Board declared:

> 1. That the means of ventilating the tunnel could have been and be so readily disconnected from the boring machine (i.e., by the movement of a single lever that would pour a stream of compressed air coming from the supply pipe

directly into the tunnel) that it has never been necessary that a single inch of cutting should have taken place in order to protect life or to secure ventilation, nor can such necessity arise in the future.

2. That in spite of the repeated orders of the Board of Trade, and the assurances of the Secretary of the Submarine Railway Company and Sir Edward Watkin himself that those orders were acquiesced in and submitted to, the substantial work of boring has nevertheless been carried to a distance of more than 600 yards from low-water mark (thus constituting a trespass on the property of the Crown).

Calling these acts "a flagrant breach of faith" on the part of the tunnel promoters, the Board of Trade wrote that henceforth the order of the court "must be strictly and literally adhered to," and that no work of maintenance, ventilation, drainage, or otherwise would be allowed without the express permission of the board. Sir Edward Watkin and his fellow directors, after some days, replied in hurt fashion to what they termed "the unjustified accusations directed against them." They reiterated their concern for the health of their employees in the tunnel, and in connection with their tunneling activities below low-water mark they came up with the ingenious explanation that "many visits of Royal and other personages have been, by request, made to the tunnel for purposes of inspection, and it was essential fully to work the machine from time to time for the purpose of such visits." They also sent a protest to Mr. Gladstone at 10 Downing Street against their hard treatment, and asked for the Prime Minister's intercession with the Board of Trade. But there was nothing doing. Mr. Gladstone politely refused to act and replied that the actions of the Board of Trade had the full sanction of the Government.

On August 5, Colonel Yolland descended once more into the tunnel to make an inspection. He found things there in a rather run-down condition. "The tunnel is not nearly so dry as it was when I first saw it," he wrote in his report to the Board of Trade, referring to the fact that the engineers had ceased work on the drainage of the gallery. Colonel Yolland also mentioned in his report that during his previous visit, on July 15, "I had an escape from what might have been a serious accident. The wet chalk in the bottom of the tunnel, between and outside the rails of the tramways, is so slippery and greasy that it is almost impossible to keep on one's feet; and, on one occasion, I suddenly slipped, and fell at full length on my back, and the back of my head came against one of the iron rails of the tramway—fortunately with no great force or my skull might have been seriously bruised or fractured." The Colonel added, "There is not light enough in the tunnel from the electric lamps to enable one to see one's way through ... so that it is necessary to carry a lamp in one hand and a note-book in the other, to record the different measurements." The Colonel then gave some startling news. He declared that, according to his measurements, somebody had advanced the length of the tunnel some seventy yards since his inspection on July 15.

When this report reached the Board of Trade, the department, outraged, made a motion before the High Court of Justice to cite the tunnel promoters for contempt. However, a cloud of doubt descended on the issue when the tunnel promoters claimed in court that Colonel Yolland's calculations were in error. The motion was put off with the promoters' promising to obey to the letter the demands of the Board of Trade. Later on in the month, Colonel Yolland, after making a further inspection, conceded that, owing to the difficulties of working in the tunnel, he had made some error of calculation. The true advance made in the tunnel since July 15, he said, was thirty-six yards—a figure he said was confirmed by the tunnel company's engineer. Colonel Yolland reported that the company engineers had installed a pump at the eastern end of the tunnel to force out the water accumulating there. He added, somewhat testily, "Of course men had to be employed in erecting this pump in the tunnel and in working it when it was ready, and as the boring machine has not been made use of for the purpose of cutting chalk, this ... conclusively proves what I had stated in my former reports, that it was not necessary to cut an inch of chalk for the purpose of ventilating and draining the tunnel."

Altogether, and with all the difficulties they had encountered, the tunnel promoters had succeeded in boring the tunnel for a distance of 2,100 yards, or a little less than a mile and a quarter, toward France. The operations at the French end, which came to a stop in March of 1883, completed 2,009 yards of pilot tunnel from the bottom of the shaft by the cliffs at Sangatte.

In the middle of August, the Government, having received all the reports from the War Office and the Board of Trade on the subject of the tunnel, caused the rival Channel-tunnel bills that had been brought before it to be set aside, and at the same time Mr. Chamberlain announced in the House of Commons that the Government had decided to propose, early the following year, the appointment of a Joint Select Committee of the House of Lords and the House of Commons to dispose of the whole tunnel question as conclusively as possible. In the meantime, he announced the Government's intention of publishing a Blue Book containing all the principal documents and correspondence concerning the tunnel. The Blue Book was issued in October, and once again the wrath of the English press fell upon the tunnel project and its promoters. The tone of the press comment was most majestically represented by an editorial in the London *Times*, which had started off the press campaign against the project the year before. The *Times* wrote that, unless it was much mistaken, "the publication of the Blue Book will be found to have closed the whole question of the Channel Tunnel for a long time to come."

> Undermined by land, overmined at sea, sluice-ridden at its entrance, and liable to asphyxiating vapors at intervals, the Tunnel will hardly be regarded by nervous travellers as a very pleasant alternative even to the horrors of seasickness....
>
> The whole system of defense must forever be at the mercy of blunderers, criminals, and madmen. It is true that we take somewhat similar risks in ordinary railway travelling, but imagination counts for a good deal in such matters, and the terrors of the Channel Tunnel under an adequate system of defense might easily affect the imagination so strongly as to render the terrors of seasickness insignificant by comparison.

Caught between the forces of claustrophobia and xenophobia, Sir Edward Watkin's great tunnel project was just about done for. In Westminster, angry citizens exhibited their feelings by smashing all the windows of the Channel Tunnel Company offices there. In the following year, the promised new investigation into the tunnel question was undertaken by a joint Parliamentary committee presided over by Lord Landsdowne. The committee met fourteen times, examined forty witnesses, and asked them fifty-three hundred and ninety-six questions. Not unexpectedly, the witnesses included Sir Garnet Wolseley, now Lord Wolseley. That Lord Wolseley in the interim had not changed his opinions on the perilous consequences of a tunnel is evident from his response to just five of the hundreds of questions put to him by the committee members.

> 5233: ... I think you said that supposing anyone in this room were to go to the barrack gates [at any of the forts at Dover at night] and to knock at the door, the door would at once be opened?—The wicket would be opened to you.
>
> 5234: Would it be the case if the person who went there had a hundred men in his company?—The man inside would not know that he had them, he would never suspect a hundred men being outside; but I would go further and say, even supposing that he would not open the barrack gates, the barrack gates are very easily knocked in.

5235: Are there any drawbridges there?—There are, but they are very seldom, if ever, drawn up in Dover.

5236: You said that if the tunnel were in existence, it would be necessary that the conditions of life in Dover should be altered; would that be one of the conditions which would be altered?—Yes.

5237: And the drawbridges would be up at night?—The drawbridges would be up at night, and nobody would be allowed to go in or out after a certain hour.

When all the evidence was in, a majority of the joint Parliamentary committee sided with the views of Lord Wolseley and voted against any Parliamentary sanction's being given to a Channel tunnel.

Sir Edward Watkin kept right on promoting his tunnel project for quite a while. By 1884—a year, incidentally, when Lord Wolseley was called away from the country to command the British expeditionary force that arrived too late at Khartoum to relieve General Gordon—Sir Edward was still doing his best to bring the British Army around to his viewpoint on the tunnel. A series of contemporary illustrations in the London illustrated weekly publication *The Graphic* records some views of a tunnel party held during that year for a group of British Army officers. One of the engravings shows a number of officers preparing to descend into the tunnel; the caption reads, "I say, Dear Chappie, if we invade France through the Tunnel, I hope I shan't be told off to lead the Advanced Guard." The visit was further reported on in an accompanying article by one of a few journalists accompanying the party. From this, it appears that the condition of the tunnel hadn't improved since the time that Colonel Yolland nearly split his head open in it. "Under foot for a great portion of the way," the author said, in describing how the visitors were drawn along the long gallery on canvas-hooded trolleys, "was ankle deep in slush," and he went on to quote from the report of one of his colleagues:

> Onward to no sound, save the splashing made by the tall workmen [who drew the trolleys] tramping through the mud and the drip, drip, drip of the water upon the hood above our heads, we are dragged and pushed ... under the bed of the Channel.... Sometimes, in the fitful flashes of light, the eye rests on falling red rivulets, like streams of blood, flowing down the damp walls. So we go on until the electric lamps cease altogether, and the long, awful cave is enveloped in a darkness that would be impenetrable but for the glimmer of a few tallow candles stuck into the bare walls of the cutting.

At the end of the tunnel the action of the boring machine was briefly demonstrated, this time by special permission of the Board of Trade, and then the party was escorted out of the tunnel and taken to a good lunch, presumably at the Lord Warden Hotel. Another engraving in the same issue of *The Graphic* shows members of the same party of officers, chairs drawn slightly back, sitting about a luncheon table. The monocled guests, ranged on each side of a clutter of bottles, potted ferns, place cards, and an interesting variety of glasses—including, as one can see fairly clearly, champagne glasses, claret glasses, and hock glasses—are being addressed by a bearded speaker. They look dazed. Yet while using his best softening-up techniques on the Army officers, Sir Edward did not let up his fire on his principal opponents among the military. Thus, during 1884, when he reintroduced his Tunnel Bill on the floor in Parliament (it was rejected by 222 votes to 84) he ridiculed the anti-tunnel generals for publicly confessing an inability to cope with defending a frontier "no bigger than the door of the House of Commons." Dealing with the question of British insularity, he also introduced the argument that since France and England had once been united as part of the same continental land mass his opponents, in refusing to unite them again, were openly showing distrust of the wisdom of Providence in having created the connection in the first place. This last assertion really incensed the editors of the London *Times*, who had been steadily invoking Providence as their ally against the tunnel all along. The *Times* ran an editorial declaring angrily that no stronger reason could be found for distrusting the whole tunnel scheme than the fact that Sir Edward had been reduced to using such an argument. The *Times* added, severely, "Ordinary people will probably be content to take the world as it appears in historic times. Everything that we possess and are—our character, our language, our freedom, our institutions, our religion, our unviolated hearths, and our far-extended Empire—we owe to the encircling sea; and when Englishmen try to penetrate the designs of Providence they will not seek them in geological speculations, but will rather thank Him Who 'isled us here.'"

Sir Edward, in his indomitable fashion, not only pursued his geological speculations but also kept pursuing the tunnel question in Parliament. In 1887, a year in which he changed the name of the Submarine Continental Railway Company to that of the Channel Tunnel Company (he had taken over the long-moribund rival company in 1886), he went on such a powerful campaign on behalf of a new Channel Tunnel Bill that it was defeated in the House by only seventy-six votes. In 1888, he tried again, and even managed to persuade Mr. Gladstone, now the leader of the Opposition, that the Channel could be tunneled under with propriety. As a result, Mr. Gladstone, in June 1888, gave his personal support to Sir Edward's Tunnel Bill and delivered a long Parliamentary speech on the subject. In this dissertation the venerable statesman, while taking nothing back about the wisdom of Providence in placing the Channel where it was, said he had now come to feel that a Channel tunnel could be used "without altering in any way our insular character or insular security, to give us some of the innocent and pacific advantages of a land frontier." But even Mr. Gladstone's support couldn't swing it. Parliament would not agree to the tunnel. At last, after all these setbacks, Sir Edward had to consider the tunnel project as a lost cause, if only temporarily. He stopped promoting it in 1894, having become involved in the meantime in a couple of alternate projects—a railway tunnel between Scotland and Ireland and a ship canal in Ireland between Dublin and Galway. Also, in 1889, he had become chairman of a company to erect at Wembley Park, near London, a great iron tower, modeled on the Eiffel Tower, which was to be known as the Watkin Tower. The Watkin Tower didn't get very high. Only a single stage was completed, and this was opened to the public in 1896; it was demolished eleven years later. Sir Edward Watkin died at Northenden, Cheshire, in 1901.

Five

THE ADVENT of the Entente Cordiale in 1904 provided the basis for the next attempt to revive the tunnel scheme. In 1907, the English Channel Tunnel Company, by now under the chairmanship of Baron Frederic Emile d'Erlanger, a banker, made another attempt to obtain Parliamentary approval for a tunnel. This time, the company had the advantage of bringing to bear on its behalf solid engineering studies and twentieth-century technology. The trains in the tunnel were now to be all electric, and the difficult task of evacuating the spoil from the tunnel during its construction was to be carried out by an ingenious new method, invented by a Frenchman named Philippe Fougerolles, of pulverizing it and mixing it with sea water into a soft slurry, then pumping the slurry out of the tunnel through pipelines. This time, while all the old arguments for and against the tunnel were being rehashed in Parliament, the tunnel promoters came up with a novel proposal designed to demonstrate the benign intentions toward England of the French Government and to allay the suspicions of the anti-tunnel faction in England. They suggested that the French end of the tunnel emerge from the side of a steep cliff on the shore of the Channel at Wissant, not far from Sangatte. The sole access to the tunnel entrance on the French side then would be made through a long horseshoe-shaped railway viaduct extending for some distance out over the sea and doubling back again to join, a mile or so away from the tunnel entrance, the French coastal rail line. Thus, the French suggested, the British fleet would be at liberty to sail up and array itself at any point offshore in a time of national emergency and at its convenience to shell the viaduct and tunnel entrance to smithereens. Expounding on the advantages of this plan in the pages of the *Revue Politique et Parlementaire*, one of the two principal architects of the 1907 tunnel plan, Albert Sartiaux—the other was the engineer, Sir Francis Fox—encouragingly pointed out that such a viaduct not only would constitute the most perfect target imaginable for the guns of the Royal Navy, but also "would be a magnificent *point de vue* for tourists." These inducements were insufficient, however. Parliament turned down the tunnel again. And a Labor M.P. declared, "If the Channel were tunneled, the Army and Navy estimates would speedily grow beyond the control of the most resolutely prudent financier. Old-age pensions would dwindle out of sight, and a shilling income tax would soon be regarded as the distant dream of an Arcadian past."

Just before the First World War, the Channel Tunnel Company, headed by Baron Frederic Emile d'Erlanger's son, Baron Emile Beaumont d'Erlanger, embarked on another crusade. In 1913, a deputation representing ninety M.P.s favorable to the tunnel scheme visited Herbert Asquith, the Prime Minister, to ask for the Government's approval for the scheme, and the

Liberal London *Daily Chronicle*, editorially proclaiming that the advent of the airplane had put an end to England's position as an island, came through with a big pro-tunnel press campaign. However, the *Times* of London continued to stick firmly to its ancient position, and it ran an editorial restating its old arguments against the tunnel and ingeniously adding a new one—that even if there were no real possibility of invasion, the very existence of the tunnel "might even itself lead to a precipitation of war, if in case of international complications it was considered necessary, in a possible moment of confusion, to close the tunnel at the Dover end." In July 1914, less than a fortnight before the outbreak of war, the Committee of Imperial Defense turned the tunnel scheme down again. But the value of a Channel tunnel as a supply route for the Allied armies on the Continent continued to be debated throughout the war, and when it was over Marshal Foch declared publicly that "If the English and the French had had a tunnel under the Channel in 1914, the war would have been shortened by at least two years." The Marshal was promptly made the honorary president of the Comité Français du Tunnel.

In postwar England, the tunnel project began to obtain heavy support in Parliament. By 1924, some four hundred M.P.s—about two-thirds of the House—were said to be for it, and the new Labor Prime Minister, Ramsay MacDonald, promised a careful and sympathetic review of the Government's position on the tunnel. He called all of the four living former Prime Ministers—Lord Balfour, Herbert Asquith, Lloyd George, and Stanley Baldwin—into consultation on the matter, as well as the Committee of Imperial Defense. The Prime Ministers met for forty minutes and rejected the scheme again, and MacDonald told Parliament that the Government felt postwar military developments had "tended, without exception, to render the Channel tunnel a more dangerous experiment" than ever. Winston Churchill protested the decision. "I do not hesitate to say that it was wrong," he told the House.

In 1929, everybody had a go at the tunnel once more, and very elaborate engineering studies were made on the subject by well-established engineering firms and were carefully examined by a special Government committee, with particular attention being given to the contention of pro-tunnel people that the construction of a Channel tunnel would provide badly needed work for Englishmen in depression times. The report of the Government's committee was, with a single dissension, favorable to the construction of the tunnel. But the Committee of Imperial Defense still was to have its say, and in May 1930 it rejected the project. This time the rejection was made primarily on two grounds, according to a high British military man who was later a member of that body. The first of these, he says, was the fear of the military that the successful construction of a Channel tunnel would so adversely affect England's Channel shipping trade that the Channel ports were likely to fall into ill repair and the harbors to start silting up—dangerous conditions in periods of national emergency; the second was their fear that if Britain became involved in another war on the Continent, the tunnel would suddenly become a traffic bottleneck through which it would be difficult to move war supplies and equipment quickly and on the massive scale required. A month after this adverse verdict by the military, a motion was nonetheless put forward in the House of Commons for approval of the tunnel, and this time such a large group of M.P.s was favorable to the scheme that the motion failed to carry by only seven votes.

For most of the thirties, the tunnel project just drifted along in a dormant state. Once every so often, when things were generally slack, the press would carry a feature story on it, and the annual meetings of the Channel Tunnel Company, still gamely presided over by Baron Emile Beaumont d'Erlanger, were always good for a paragraph tucked somewhere into the financial pages under mildly mocking headlines, such as "Hope Eternal," "The Channel Tunnel Again," or, in one of the popular dailies, just "The Poor Old Tunnel."

The outbreak of the Second World War, however, far from putting the Channel tunnel completely out of sight, revived the issue, for a time, anyway. In November 1939 the French Chamber of Deputies passed a resolution calling for the construction of a tunnel; early in 1940, Prime Minister Neville Chamberlain—the son, incidentally, of Joseph Chamberlain, who as president of the Board of Trade had ordered the tunnel workings stopped back in the eighties—turned the tunnel project down again in a parliamentary reply. The retreat from Dunkirk gave pro-tunnel and anti-tunnel people the opportunity of putting forth their arguments about the tunnel once more, with some variations—with the pro-tunnelers claiming that a Channel tunnel might have enabled the British Expeditionary Force to keep a bridgehead in France, and the anti-tunnelers countering that the same tunnel would have given German paratroopers the opportunity of seizing the English end and using it as a bridgehead for the invasion of England.

Then, after the fall of France, when the Germans were busily making preparations for the invasion of England, the question arose among the British military as to whether the enemy might not just possibly attempt to reach England by surreptitiously tunneling underneath the Channel. As a consequence, the War Office called in an eminent British civil engineer, the late Sir William Halcrow, and asked him to make a study of the question of whether the Germans could pull off such a feat. "We examined the situation quite carefully and concluded that, provided we kept reasonably alert, the Germans could not dig the tunnel without being detected," an engineering colleague of Sir William Halcrow's on the survey said a while ago. He added, "Their difficulty would lie in the disposal of the spoil. They couldn't get rid of it without our seeing from the air that something peculiar was going on. If they tried to dump the spoil into the sea at night it would have to be done at the turn of the tide, and the chalk would leave a cloud in the sea that would not be dissipated by daylight. If they pulverized the spoil, converted it into a slurry, and pumped it well out to sea, we would be able to spot the chalk cloud too, and even if they tried other means of dispersing the spoil the very process of dispersal would call for such extensive installations that we would soon be on to them."

In 1942, somebody at the War Office had another look into the tunnel situation, this time for the purpose of finding out if it would be practical for the British to start tunneling under the Channel—the idea presumably being the creation of a supply route to France ahead of an Allied invasion, with the last leg of the route being completed once the Allied Armies had installed themselves on the French coast. Again, several prominent British civil engineers were called into consultation, but the subject was abruptly dropped, without investigation of the problem of disposing of the spoil, when the engineers estimated that a tunnel probably would take eight years to complete—three years longer than the war then was expected to last.

From 1940 on, the British kept a routine watch on their reconnaissance photographs for signs of tunneling on the French side, especially around the site of the still existing shaft of the French Tunnel Company at Sangatte. Early in 1944, R.A.F. and U.S.A.F. reconnaissance showed signs of unusual installations being made near Sangatte, but these later turned out to be unconnected with subterranean workings. As it happened, they were launching sites for V-2 bombs.

The actual handling by the Germans of the old tunnel shaft during the occupation of France was rather peculiar. Far from trying to continue the existing tunnel in the early part of the Occupation, they treated it in contemptuous fashion, 96 using the shaft as a dump for old chunks of machinery, used shell casings, bits of rubbish, and broken slabs of concrete. Later on, their attitude changed drastically. They sealed the top of the shaft with a poured-concrete platform. Then, in weirdly romantic fashion, they built a large rim of fitted stone around the platform to create an ornamental-wall effect, and added around the well a grass-and-flagstone terrace complete with formal walks and sets of monumental-looking stone steps laid out in symmetrical style. Apparently their notion was to bring the tunnel aesthetically into harmony with a military cemetery they installed between the tunnel entrance and the sea.

After the war, the Channel-tunnel project continued to languish in prewar fashion. If anything, even less than before was heard in the press about the activities of the Channel Tunnel Company. The company's headquarters at the Southern Railway offices at London Bridge were blown up in the blitz, and all the company's records were destroyed. For some time, while attempts were made to piece together duplicate lists from Government files, the Channel Tunnel Company didn't even know who the majority of its stockholders were, but that didn't matter too much, considering the circumstances. Baron Emile Beaumont d'Erlanger, the chairman, had died in 1939, and his place on the Board was taken by his nephew, Leo d'Erlanger, also a banker. Leo d'Erlanger, now a spry, elegant, silver-haired gentleman in his sixties, brightly confesses to having had little interest in the tunnel until about twelve years ago. "I was brought up in a home where the Channel tunnel was a family religion, and, to tell the truth, I didn't give it too much thought," he says. "My grandfather used to talk about it when I came back for the holidays from Eton. 'Politics,' they all used to say. 'The only reason why the tunnel isn't built is politics.' I never paid much attention. I thought it was an old dodo and never had anything to do with it in my Uncle Emile's lifetime. When he died and I took over, I used to look forward with dread to the annual general meetings. I had nothing to say. I considered the whole thing moribund. For a few years we met, I remember, at the Charing Cross Hotel, which belonged to the Southern Railway [a successor to Sir Edward Watkin's South-Eastern Railway], and the secretary was an elderly retired man by the name of Cramp, who once had something to do with the Southern Railway, I think. We used to have difficulty in getting a quorum. I suppose we would manage to get four or five people to turn up."

However, the lost-cause atmosphere began to undergo a change in 1948, when Sir Herbert Walker, the former general manager of the Southern Railway, which was taken over by British Railways in the nationalization program of that year, acted temporarily as chairman of the Channel Tunnel Company. Walker came to believe that the Channel-tunnel scheme could be a practical one in the postwar era, and he brought it to life again. Largely as a result of his persuasions, a Parliamentary study group began to look into the tunnel question once more, and the Channel Tunnel Company's lobbyists once more set about building up pro-tunnel opinion among M.P.s. It was just like old times for the pro-tunnelers, but with one significant difference. By the mid-fifties, it became clear that in the emerging age of rockets bearing nuclear warheads the traditional strategic arguments of the British military against the construction of a Channel tunnel would no longer have the same force that they had once had. And as for the old fears of military conscription in peacetime and high taxes, they had long ago been realized without a tunnel. It was therefore an event to make the hearts of all pro-tunnelers beat fast when, one day in February 1955, in the House of

Commons, Harold Macmillan, then Minister of Defense, in answer to a parliamentary question as to whether the Government would have objections of a military nature to raise against a Channel tunnel, replied, "Scarcely at all."

This seemed like a green light to D'Erlanger, but for a while he couldn't quite decide what to do after seeing it flash on. Early in 1956, however, he went to see Paul Leroy-Beaulieu, who was a director of the French Tunnel Company—the Société Concessionnaire du Chemin de Fer Sous-marin entre la France et l'Angleterre—and the grandson of Michel Chevalier, who had founded the company in 1875. D'Erlanger suggested that, since the tunnel was a common ancestral interest, the two of them have another try at promoting it. Leroy-Beaulieu agreed, and he suggested that as the Suez Canal Company's concession in Egypt was due to run out in 1968, and might not be renewed, the Suez Company might possibly be interested in turning to a Channel tunnel as its next project. Sure enough, the principals of the Suez Company, whose headquarters were in Paris, were interested in the idea, but the sudden seizure of the Canal by Colonel Nasser in July of that year kept them too distracted to pursue the tunnel project just then. In the meantime, quite independently of these tunnel developments in Paris and London, two young international lawyers in New York, Frank Davidson and Cyril Means, Jr., became intrigued by the possibility of a tunnel between England and France. Davidson and Means happened to have good connections in Wall Street, and after they established contact with the two existing tunnel companies by letter, Means went over to London and Paris early in February of 1957 to investigate the tunnel situation and to offer the tunnel people there—and the Suez Canal Company—the chance of obtaining some substantial American financial backing for the construction of a tunnel if it proved to be a practical proposition. The tunnel people in Europe showed varying degrees of interest in the proposal, and to strengthen their position, Davidson and Means, with another friend, an engineer, Arnaud de Vitry d'Avancourt, formed a New York corporation called Technical Studies, Inc., with the announced purpose of financing technical investigations and promoting the construction of a Channel tunnel.

In April 1957, the Suez Canal Company, which by then had given up any hope of regaining control of the Canal, jumped into the tunnel picture by announcing that it intended to collaborate with the English and French tunnel companies to have made a very detailed geological survey of the Channel bed to determine the practicability of a tunnel. The tunnel came into the news again. When, at the seventy-sixth annual meeting of the Channel Tunnel Company, in London, D'Erlanger got up to confirm the latest development, he did so not before the usual handful of disillusioned shareholders, but in a room packed with people who had suddenly rediscovered and dusted off old Channel Tunnel Company stock certificates. A correspondent from the *Times* of London who was present reported of the stockholders' reaction to the speech of the company's chairman on the possibilities of seriously reviving the tunnel project that it took only a few minutes "to excite their minds to a pleasurable pitch" and that "at least one member of Mr. d'Erlanger's audience darted out in the middle of his speech to instruct his broker to buy in shares." According to the *Times*, the only note of doubt was struck by a stockholder at the end of the meeting, which lasted half an hour:

> Mr. John Elliott, who bought his shares for a song almost, asked where the company's workings were. Did they really exist? He had visited Dover, and neither police, shopkeepers, nor the county surveyor could tell him where they were. He suggested that the board prove their existence by escorting a nominated half-dozen shareholders on an eye-witness excursion.

Little attention was paid to the objector. The *Times* reported that "other shareholders pooh-poohed his scepticism," and the meeting broke up. It was a far cry from the days of Sir Edward Watkin's special trains to Dover for tunnel parties. However, the price of Channel Tunnel Company stock, which had been available for years on the London Stock Exchange for as low as sixpence, rose to more than ten shillings by the day of the meeting and shortly thereafter rose rapidly, until by May 20 it reached twenty-six shillings and ninepence—six shillings and ninepence more than the price of the first Channel Tunnel Company stock in 1876.

The British press, on the whole, reacted to the latest tunnel development in tolerant fashion. There was, however, a spirited discussion of the subject in an article in the *Daily Telegraph* in the spring of 1957, marked by an attack on the whole scheme by Major-General Sir Edward Spears. General Spears wrote that although powerful interests now appeared to be backing the construction of a Channel tunnel, the objections raised to the project in the past were as valid as ever. "Such a tunnel would bind this island to the Continent irrevocably [and] would soon link our fate to that of our Continental neighbors," he asserted, and he added that if the new scheme were persisted in, steps should be taken to enlighten the public before the Government was committed to approving it. General Spears's position was supported by Lord Montgomery. Choosing Trafalgar Day as the most appropriate time to express himself on the subject, Lord Montgomery said at a Navy League luncheon in October of 1957, "There is talk these days of a Channel tunnel. Strategically it would weaken us. Why give up one of our greatest assets—our island home—and make things easier for our enemies?

The Channel tunnel is a wildcat scheme and I am wholeheartedly opposed to it.... I hope that the Navy League will have nothing to do with it."

However, by Trafalgar Day the pro-tunnelers were hard at it, too. In July 1957, the four main interests involved in the scheme—the English and French Channel-tunnel companies, the Suez Canal Company and Technical Studies—had combined to create an organization called the Channel Tunnel Study Group to contract for modern technical surveys of the whole tunnel question. The new group is said to have spent over a million dollars on having these surveys made. The studies included a very detailed survey of the Channel bed with modern electronic geophysical equipment and deep rock borings and sea-bottom samples made across the neck of the Channel, as well as microscopic examination of these rock samples to determine their microfossil composition and probable position in the strata from which they were taken. Curiously enough, while the geological survey was under way, somebody on the project took the trouble to inquire into the old French hydrographic surveys for a Channel tunnel, and after some diligent searching he turned up, in a dusty waiting room of a disused Paris suburban railroad station, where it had been stored for an age, a collection of thousands of the sea-bottom samples made in the French Channel-tunnel surveys of 1875 and 1876. All of the samples were found neatly packed away in test tubes and ticketed, and the searchers even uncovered a case of the geological specimens that Thomé de Gamond himself had recovered in 1855 by his naked plunges to the bottom of the Channel in the neighborhood of the Varne. The geologists weren't interested in going by way of the Varne any more, but many of the old 1875-76 samples were taken away for microfossil examination as part of a check on how the results of the old surveys compared with the new. Except for some variations relating to the extent of the cretaceous outcrop in the middle of the Channel, the findings tallied nicely.

The new Study Group had a number of other elaborate surveys made, too, on the economic and engineering problems involved in the creation and operation of a Channel tunnel or an equivalent means of cross-Channel transport. Besides developing plans for a bored tunnel—the projected double-rail tunnel, interconnected at intervals by cross-passages, is essentially a modern version of William Low's plan of the 1860s, with an extra small service tunnel being added between the main tunnels—the Study Group's engineering consultants developed in detail schemes for a Channel bridge, an immersed railway tube, an immersed road tube, a combined immersed tube with two railway tracks, and a four-way road system on two levels. The bridge proposed would be an enormous affair with approximately 142 piers and with four main spans in the center of the Strait each 984 feet long. These spans would tower a maximum of 262½ feet above sea level to allow the largest ships in the world to pass underneath with plenty of room to spare. The bridge would take no longer to build than a road tunnel, but it would cost about twice as much, and in addition it would be expensive and difficult to maintain and would present a hazard to navigation. The immersed tube proposed for either rail or road traffic (but not both) probably would cost about the same as a bored tunnel and might be constructed in four years. A combined road-rail tube would take about the same time to build, but would be more expensive even than a bridge. Among the best-known schemes for a combined tube is that of a Frenchman, André Basdevant, who has proposed one with a four-lane highway and a two-track rail line. This scheme would pretty much run along the old Cap Gris-Nez-Folkestone route of Thomé de Gamond, and it would even have, like most of Thomé de Gamond's schemes, an artificial island in mid-channel on the Varne. As for the latest scheme for a laid, rather than a bored, tube, it would be no different from Thomé de Gamond's plan in 1834 for a submerged tube, and as in that old plan a trench would be dug, by operations conducted at the surface, across the Channel bottom to receive the tube, which would be prefabricated in sections and towed out to sea to be laid down in the trench a section at a time. This time the digging of the trench would be carried out from a huge above-surface working platform, something like an aircraft-carrier deck on sets of two-hundred-foot-high stilts, that would jack itself up and move on across the Channel as the work progressed. From these and other surveys, the Study Group concluded by March 1960 that the best means of linking Britain and France would be by a rail tunnel, either bored or immersed, which, while avoiding the difficult ventilation problems of a long road tunnel, would make for convenient transport of cars and trucks by a piggyback system. It further proposed that the tunnel be operated jointly by the British and French Government-run railways under a long lease from an international company yet to be formed, and that only the bare tunnel itself be privately financed, with the British and French state-run railways providing the installations, terminals, and rolling stock at a cost of some twenty million pounds.

When D'Erlanger announced the Study Group's proposals, calling all the latest tunnel laborings "a last glorious effort to get this through," the British press received the news with big headlines on the front pages but with considerable indignation on its editorial pages. The core of the objections was not of a military nature but had to do with the number of financial concessions that the tunnel people were asking from the British and French Governments (that is, taxpayers) as a basis for going ahead with the scheme. The general attitude of the press was that the British Government should have nothing to do with some of the financial concessions asked. There were a good many references, all very familiar to a reader of the press attacks during the tunnel uproar back in the eighties, to "promoters," and the tone of editorial reaction was fairly well typified by a sarcastic article in *The Economist* entitled "Pie Under the Sea." And the *Times* ran an editorial declaring snappily that, as the proposals stood, "the light at the end of the tunnel would be either bright gold for the private owners of the £20 million of equity capital or Bright Red for the Anglo-French taxpayer." Then, shortly afterward, the tunnel came under public attack by Eoin C. Mekie, chairman of Silver City Airways, which in the years since the Second World War has ferried more than three hundred thousand cars and a million and a half passengers by air to and from the Continent. Mekie denounced the tunnel scheme as "commercial folly" and described it as "a feat of engineering which is already made obsolete by the speed of modern technical advances." Other attacks were made, too, from the enthusiasts over the future of Hovercraft, the heavier-than-air craft, still in the experimental stage, which ride on a cushion of air; and from, not unexpectedly, Channel shipping and ferry interests. Then Viscount Montgomery, in a newspaper interview, returned to the attack on the tunnel on the ground of its undermining what he called "our island strategy." He also observed in particular, when asked about the feasibility of blowing the tunnel up in case of war or threatened war, "The lessons of history show that things that ought to be blown up never are, as Guy Fawkes discovered." And Major-General Spears in the spring of 1960 gave fuller vent to his anti-tunnel views in a pamphlet that he wrote and had circulated privately. Its general tenor was set by General Spears's assertion that "the Channel saved us in 1940 and may well save us again," and that "The British people need no tunnels." And he asked, "Who would have believed that in the last war the Germans would not have destroyed the enormously important bridge over the Rhine at Remagen? But they failed to do so."

To all such criticism as this, the Channel-tunnel people reacted not with the kind of broadsides that Sir Edward Watkin would have let loose in the heyday of the Channel-tunnel controversy but by hiring a public-relations outfit headed by a man called E. D. O'Brien, a former publicity director for the Conservative party, who is said to be known among his colleagues as Champagne Toby. O'Brien's champagne appears to be weaker stuff than Sir Edward Watkin's; the pro-tunnel publicity his outfit puts out seems to consist of things like a small booklet called "Channel Tunnel, the Facts," which an O'Brien assistant has described as "a sort of child's guide, in Q. and A. form, you know, about the tunnel."

As soon as the British press fell on the promoters for making the demands they did for Government financial guarantees, the promoters came up with a set of counter-proposals. They offered to finance not only the tunnel itself but also the terminals and approaches on both sides; they further proposed leasing the tunnel directly to the two governments, thus avoiding the earlier requirement of governmental guarantee of the bonds.

When the subject of constructing a Channel tunnel will come up for a decision one way or the other before the British Cabinet and Parliament again nobody seems willing to predict, and what the Cabinet will decide nobody seems willing to predict, either. However, D'Erlanger, who says that he would consider another tunnel thumbs down by the British Government or Parliament "a negation of progress," is always happy to talk about the benefits a Channel tunnel would confer upon Europe. "You have fifty million people on this side of the Channel and two hundred million plus on the Continental side. If you join them by a small hyphen, I think it *must* facilitate trade on both sides," he says. "I like to think of the tunnel as a kind of engagement ring that would bind Britain's Outer Seven into a workable marriage with the six countries of the Common Market. Think of shipping goods from Rome to Birmingham or from Edinburgh to Bordeaux without breaking bulk, and at half the cost! It's high time Europe had a manifestation of progress along the lines of the St. Lawrence Seaway, and I think a Channel tunnel would be the great civil-engineering feat of the century for Europe."

In the meantime, with all the brave words, and all the money poured into the project, the Channel Tunnel Company still has something of a phantom air about it. It doesn't have a regular staff—D'Erlanger is a busy City banker—and it has no real office of its own. D'Erlanger's banking headquarters are at the investment house of which he is a partner, Philip Hill, Higginson, Erlangers, Ltd., along Moorgate, but no Channel Tunnel Company records are kept there. The nearest thing to a headquarters for the Channel Tunnel Company is a set of Victorian offices on Broad Street Place, in the City, occupied by a firm of "secretaries" called W. H. Stentiford & Co. These offices are reached by a very ancient and slow ironwork-gate lift, and a sign in the corridor shows that W. H. Stentiford & Co. is the representative of an astonishing variety of companies, including the Channel Tunnel Company, Ltd., and a number of outfits with such exotic corporate names as the Tea Share Trust, Ltd., Uruwira Minerals, Ltd., Dominion Keep (Klerksdorp, Ltd.), and Klerksdorp Consolidated Goldfields, Ltd. Inside, amid a clutter of ticking clocks, great ledgers, old safes emblazoned with peeling coats of arms, great piles of papers, and trays of teacups, a small staff of round-shouldered retainers toils away vicariously over the affairs of these far-flung organizations—making up accounts and annual or quarterly statements, filling out and recording stock certificates, answering letters, and so on. All this clerkly activity is presided over by an eminently respectable and precisely mannered man by the name of P. S. Elliston, who also arranges board meetings for his many client companies in a room set aside at Stentiford's for the purpose. Mr. Elliston's organization "took on" the Channel Tunnel

Company in the early forties, and all its annual meetings since 1947 have been held at Stentiford's, with Mr. Elliston present in his capacity of representative of his firm of secretaries. Mr. Elliston finds things changed a bit from the time when the Channel Tunnel Company first became one of his firm's clients. In those old days, he says, the whole annual meeting could generally be disposed of in between five and ten minutes, with only a couple of directors being present—Mr. Elliston having thoughtfully bought one share of Channel Tunnel Company stock to enable himself to vote in case no other shareholder besides a couple of directors could be persuaded to turn up to make a quorum of three. Now, he says, it may sometimes take twenty-five minutes or even as long as forty-five minutes to transact necessary business. As for Channel Tunnel Company stock, it has fluctuated all the way from sixpence to fifty shillings—its price one day in 1959 at a time when the company's balance sheet showed a cash balance of just £161. The price of the stock at the time this book was written was about twenty-two shillings, and the company's cash in hand (in 1961 it issued a little more stock to keep going) was £91,351 "and a few shillings." Owing to the wartime destruction of its records and the difficulty of tracking down all the old transactions, the Channel Tunnel Company still doesn't know who all its stockholders are, and, conversely, there are quite a few people scattered about who probably aren't aware that they are company stockholders.

Mr. Elliston describes the last fifteen years or so of the company's history as containing "several periods where there was very keen interest" in the tunnel scheme, especially in 1957 and 1958, with Stentiford's being subjected, he says, to "a persistent spate of enquiries," including calls from newspaper reporters and letters from schoolboys asking why the tunnel was never built.

Some time ago, when I was in England, I decided to take a trip down to the coast between Folkestone and Dover to the scene of the violent tunnel controversy of the eighties. I had heard that the shaft of the old Shakespeare Cliff gallery in which Sir Edward Watkin did so much of his promoting and entertaining, as well as tunneling, had been sealed off many years ago, but I was aware that the Abbots Cliff gallery, or part of it, still existed. Through the good offices of Leo d'Erlanger and Harold J. B. Harding, the vice-president of the Institution of Civil Engineers, who has directed many of the latest technical surveys on the proposed Channel tunnel, I arranged to go down one day from London to Folkestone and to be taken into the old Abbots Cliff tunnel. Written permission had to be obtained from the Government for the visit, and the necessary arrangements had to be made well in advance with officials of British Railways, the present owner, representing the Crown, of the coastal lands once the domain of Sir Edward Watkin's South-Eastern Railway Company. Harding explained to me that since the tunnel entrance was kept locked up and lay in a not readily accessible part of the cliffs facing the sea, it would be practical for me to make the visit only under fairly good weather conditions, and then under the escort of people equipped with lamps and the means of opening up the tunnel entrance. "You may get a bit wet and a bit dirty, so don't wear a good suit," Harding added, and he went on to say that he had seen to it that I would be shown around the tunnel by a civil engineer named Kenneth W. Adams, from the district office of British Railways at Ashford, Kent—Adams being, in Harding's words, "a keen engineer who has become something of a hobbyist on the old tunnel workings."

Wearing an old suit, I duly took a train early one fair morning in autumn, from Charing Cross, and when I got off at Folkestone Central Station, Adams, a stocky, cheerful man who seemed to be about forty, was waiting for me. He had a little car waiting outside the station, and when he got into it, he introduced me to an assistant sitting in the driver's seat named Jack Burgess. "Jack's grandfather was a surface worker at the tunnel workings at Shakespeare Cliff," Adams said as Burgess started the car up. "Jack was just telling me that he remembers his grandfather telling him, when he was a boy, about Lord Palmerston coming down to visit the tunnel in 1881. The old chap remembered that the food that was brought into the tunnel for parties of visitors from the Lord Warden Hotel at Dover came in hay boxes—that is, in big wicker boxes interlined with a thick layer of hay to keep the food warm."

Burgess drove us through the outer part of Folkestone toward the sea at a pretty good clip, with the little car buzzing away like a high-speed sewing machine, and in a very little time, after climbing up a long, gentle slope by the back of the cliffs, we drew up on the heights of East Cliff, a kind of promontory within Eastwear Bay, which lies to the north-east of Folkestone Harbor. There, in two broad curves to the left and right of us, the precipitous face of the white chalk cliffs gleamed, like huge ruined walls with grassed-over rubble piled about their base, in hazy sunlight. Far below us, and stretching away into the haze, lay the Channel, gray and, for the time being, pretty calm. A hundred feet or so from where our car stopped was a massive round stone tower, its sides tapering in toward the top like a child's sand castle; two similar towers lay some distance from us in the direction of Folkestone. These, Adams explained, were Martello towers, formerly cannon-bearing fortifications that were installed in prominent places all along the Dover-Folkestone coastal area during the invasion scares early in the nineteenth century to repel surprise landings by the troops of Napoleon Bonaparte. (The three Martello towers comprised the main artillery defenses of Folkestone Harbor even as late in the century as the time of the great tunnel controversy in the eighties.) Then he pointed to the cliffs stretching to the north-east. "You see that large white building on top of the cliff almost at the very end of the bay? That's Abbots Cliff, and the tunnel is at the base of it," he said. "We'll take you down that way in a couple of minutes, but first I'd like to show you something that may interest you."

We walked a short distance down a path by East Cliff to a point where we could see, as we couldn't previously, the rail line that ran along the coast, partly through rail tunnels piercing the cliffs, and partly over the land that rose above their base. Then Adams pointed out to me something jutting horizontally out of the chalk cliffs a little above and to the side of the railroad cutting. It was a large and long-rusted collection of wheels, gears, and cams, all compounded together into the shape of some fantastic Dadaist engine. "What you see there is the remains of the last machine ever tried out for boring a Channel tunnel," Adams said. "That's the Whittaker boring machine, an electrically driven affair, powered by a steam-driven generator, and it was tried out here after the First World War. Actually, it was developed by the Royal Engineers for mining under the German lines, and in 1919 Sir Percy Tempest, who was chief engineer of the South East & Chatham Railway—an amalgamation of the South-Eastern Railway and the London, Chatham & Dover Railway, which in turn, by further amalgamation with other lines, became the Southern Railway—thought it might do for the Channel tunnel. In 1919 he asked permission from the Board of Trade to drive a new heading from the old Number Three ventilating shaft at the eastern end of Shakespeare Cliff a little way under the foreshore, and got it, but he changed his mind and decided to try the machine in the chalk down here. The Whittaker machine cut a tunnel twelve feet in diameter, and some time between 1921 and 1924 they drove a heading into the chalk, just at the point where it's sticking out now, for some four hundred feet. They never quite removed the machine from the heading when they were finished, but it was maintained right up to the outbreak of the Second World War, when it became derelict."

Adams and I walked back to the car. As we did so, he revealed himself as being pro-tunnel. "It's a tragic thing, this tunnel business, I think. If the tunnel had been built forty or fifty years ago, just think of what an asset to Europe it would have been," he said. We packed ourselves in, and Burgess drove us down a very rough, narrow road to the level of the railroad line. There, by a maintenance shed, a small, thin workman was waiting for us. He was wearing an old cloth peaked cap, a white duffel coat, and rubber knee boots, and by his feet he had ready-lighted Tilley lamps—similar in appearance to miners' lamps but operated by kerosene under pressure, like a Primus stove. Adams and Burgess jumped out of the car, and Burgess unlocked and opened up the rear trunk. I got out of the car, too. Then the workman, whom Adams addressed as Jim, disappeared briefly into the shed and came out with a pile of knee boots, which he began flinging into the car trunk. "We'll be needing these," Adams remarked to me. Next Jim brought out an enormous wrench, at least two feet long, and slung that on top of the protesting rubber boots, and then he came up with an armful of duffel coats, which he handed around. We put them on and all of us got into the car; the little workman wordlessly, with a wide gaptoothed grin, squeezed into the back seat with me and settled back with the two big lighted Tilley lamps on his lap. The lamps gave off a gentle roaring sound, like subdued blowtorches, and they gave off heat that warmed the whole back of the car.

We drove off down a narrow, steep, tortuously winding, and very rugged road, through a kind of wilderness of concrete rubble and piles of old heavy wooden construction beams, toward the base of the cliffs, and when we finally got there, we continued along the wide top of a concrete sea wall for a considerable distance until the wall suddenly narrowed and the car could go no farther.

We all got out, and Adams, Burgess, and I took off our shoes and put on the knee boots that Burgess got out of the trunk; and, with Jim and Burgess leading the way and bearing between them the glowing Tilley lamps and the giant wrench, we continued on foot along the sea wall, now as narrow as the sidewalk of a small city street. The chalk cliffs towered perhaps a couple of hundred feet above us. "The tunnel is about three-quarters of a mile ahead along the sea wall," Adams remarked as he walked beside me, and as we went along he explained that his primary job at British Railways was the design of sea defenses between Folkestone and Dover to combat erosion. "It's a good job you didn't pick a later time in the year to visit the tunnel," he went on. "This sea wall would hardly be negotiable on foot when the water's rough, and in winter, with the sou'westers blowing in especially, we have some real shockers."

After another fifteen minutes or so of walking along an area where the cliffs rose back beyond a sort of terrace formed by old landslides—the railway line ran along this terrace in the open—Adams told me that the tunnel entrance was not far off. A few hundred feet farther on, we finally reached it—a small recessed place in the grassy rubble at the base of the cliff terrace and, set into it, a four-foot-square door of rough, thick wood encased by a frame of very old and very heavy timbers. The door was hinged with heavy gate hinges and secured not by a padlock but by a very large metal nut, which Jim now attacked with his great wrench.

As he wrestled with it, Adams, smiling, remarked that the entrance wasn't a very big one, considering the size of the Channel-tunnel project. "I once brought a Canadian executive, a rather impressive-looking fellow, down here by request, in '57, I think it was," he recalled. "It seemed very important to him to inspect the entrance to the tunnel. When I took him along the sea wall and showed him this entrance, he took a look at it and just burst out laughing. I asked him what was up. He went on laughing, and finally he told me why. He said he was employed by a large American oil company, and that his company had sent him over here to spy out the possibility of buying up land for filling stations near the entrance to the proposed Channel tunnel. Actually, of course, nobody knows precisely where a new tunnel would come out on the English side, and it would be very doubtful whether they would make use of any of the old workings."

The little workman unloosened the nut, and, with various groans and creaks, the door to the tunnel allowed itself to be pulled and shouldered open. Then, one by one, we stooped down and entered the tunnel through the small opening. When my eyes adjusted themselves from the light of day to the light of the Tilley lamps we had brought with us, I found that we were standing in a square-timbered heading perhaps six feet high and about the same in width. The floor, like the roof, was timbered, and from the roof, as well as from parts of the sides of the heading, a pale fungus growth drooped down. The atmosphere was pretty dank. Just inside the entrance, either hanging from big rough nails protruding from the wooden walls or lying to one side on the floor, there was a clutter of various objects—rusty chains, augers, lengths of decaying rope, candles, and a couple of lobster pots, the presence of which Adams explained to me. "They get washed up from time to time, and our lads, when they find them, put them in here for safekeeping," he said. Slowly we made our way into the tunnel. There was room for a set of narrow-gauge rail tracks, but most of the thin rails had been torn up, and a number of them lay piled to our right by the wall. On the left, untracked and abandoned, lay one of the rail trolleys that obviously had been used for hauling out spoil. The little rusted wheels on which it rested were of clearly Victorian design, with spokes elaborately arranged in curlicued fashion. "This is the access heading we're in," Adams told me as we found our way along, heads down. "The chalk carted out from the Beaumont boring machine was taken through here and dumped right into the sea outside the entrance. But this access heading wasn't the first to be built; it was dug by hand from the direction in which we're going, from the bottom of a vertical shaft sunk from the level of the South-Eastern Railway line seventy-four feet up above this concrete lining we're coming to now. As you see—" Adams took a Tilley lamp from Burgess and flashed it on the roof of the concrete lining—"the shaft has been closed up long ago. Now we'll go on. This first stretch is taking us in a northerly direction."

After going a short distance, we came to another concrete lining. This, Adams said, was to reinforce the tunnel at the point where it passed underneath the railway line. We went on again, this time walking on a dirt floor, and then we came to a timbered junction, from which the tunnel branched off again to the right in the north-east direction that was originally intended to bring it into line with the gallery at Shakespeare Cliff, while to the left there was a low-roofed chamber that probably once housed a siding and a maintenance workshop for the Beaumont boring machine. Then, walking now on half-rotted planks, in the warm light of the restlessly moving Tilley lamps, we entered the circular, unlined tunnel of Lower Chalk—a smooth, light-gray cavern, seven feet in diameter, that stretched far ahead to disappear into darkness. Our footing was slippery, and a small stream of water ran in the direction from which we had come in a rough gutter cut in the chalk, but the tunnel at this point seemed surprisingly dry for a hole that had lain unlined for some eighty years, and the stream of water draining away didn't seem to me to be really any greater than the one in the Orangeburg pipe that drains seepage from under the cellar of my summer house in Connecticut.

We had gone only a little way along the chalk tunnel when Adams, walking ahead of me, began flashing his light along the wall and then stopped and motioned me to come and look at the spot where he had focused his lamp. I did so and saw, cut into the chalk in crude lettering, the following inscription:

THIS
TUNNEL
WAS
BUGN
IN
1880
WILLIAM SHARP

However, this was not exactly how the inscription went, for its author, after finishing it, obviously had decided that "BUGN" didn't look right, and, being unable to erase the incision, he had had another go at it, inscribing the second try to one side and partly over the first, so that the intended "begun" now came out like "BEGUBNUGN." But with all the crudeness of the inscription, the author had been careful with the lettering, even to point of conscientiously incising serifs on the "T"s and "E"s.

While the light played about the inscription, I could see clearly, on the tunnel face, the ringlike marks left by individual revolutions of the cutting head of the Beaumont boring machine. After a few moments we moved on again, and eventually, after trudging over ground that became increasingly slippery, we came to a point where some of the chalk had given way, filling the tunnel about a quarter of the way up with debris. Adams said that the going got a bit better later on but that we were likely to find ourselves in water over our knee boots if we went any farther. At that point, impressed with the sight of all the fallen rock about and by the realization that we were in a seven-foot hole at least a quarter of a mile inside a huge cliff on a deserted stretch of coast, I felt as though I had seen enough. I suddenly realized what a smart idea Sir Edward Watkin had had in providing visitors with that champagne lift while they were well under the sea. So we turned back again and slowly, in silence, made our way out of Sir Edward's first tunnel.

When I stepped through the tunnel entrance into the light, it seemed very noisy outside. Sea gulls were shrieking overhead, and the Channel waves were roaring and heaving insistently. I had a slight headache, and I mentioned this to Adams. "Oh, yes, I have the same thing," he said. "Although the air in the tunnel is remarkably fresh, considering the length of time it's been locked up and the fact that there's only one entrance, there isn't quite as much oxygen in it as one might want." Jim began to lock up the entrance again, and while he was doing so, Adams suggested that we might see if we could spot the entrance shaft on the plateau above us. We climbed up the cliffside, and after a while we located it, a filled-in depression resting in a mass of bramble bushes. We waded through the bushes and stood over the remains of Number One shaft, still feeling a bit headachy. As we stood there, we picked and ate a few blackberries still left on the bushes from summer. "They're quite good," Adams said.

After we had had some lunch in Folkestone, Adams suggested that before I went back to London I might want to take a look at the site of the old Number Two shaft and the main tunnel at Shakespeare Cliff, even though the Number Two shaft and the Number Three ventilating shaft had been long ago closed up. I was agreeable to that, and Burgess drove us, by way of Dover, to a point along a back road, from which we could walk to the top of Shakespeare Cliff from the land side. While Burgess stayed in the little car, Adams and I set off up a long slope to the cliff head, walking along the edge of a harrowed field, the soil of which seemed to be riddled with the kind of large flints typical of the Upper Chalk layer.

On the way up, Adams told me what had happened to the main tunnel and shaft after the workings were finally stopped by the Board of Trade. "Everything stopped dead at the tunnel workings until 1892," Adams said. "By then, Sir Edward Watkin knew he was beaten on the Channel tunnel, so he tried a different kind of tunneling, and the South-Eastern Railway engineers began boring for coal a matter of a few yards away from the tunnel shaft. They went down to 2,222 feet with their boring, at which level they met a four-foot seam of good-quality coal, and the company obtained authority by an act of Parliament to mine for coal under the foreshore. As for the Channel-tunnel shaft itself, it was abandoned in 1902 and filled up with breeze—ashes and slag—from the colliery, and the Number Three ventilation shaft at the eastern end of Shakespeare Cliff was also filled with breeze in the same year. But the colliery never paid off any better than the tunnel project. It ran into trouble around 1907 or 1908, and then the owners decided they'd have a try at getting iron ore out of the workings, and so all the mineral mining rights were bought by the Channel Steel Company, but the iron mining didn't prosper any more than the coal mining. The Channel Steel Company went into voluntary liquidation in 1952, and all the mining rights passed to the original freeholders, who are now the British Government."

Adams and I climbed over a wooden fence stile, and after a couple of more minutes of uphill walking we arrived at the top of Shakespeare Cliff. We approached to a point near the edge and kneeled in the tall grass, buffeted by a strong afternoon wind that struck us squarely in the face. It was a magnificent view. The Channel lay very far below us, and although I could not see the coast of France because of the haze—Adams said that on a fine day anybody could see clearly the clock tower outside Boulogne—I could see shipping scudding along in whitecaps in the middle of the Strait. To the left of us, not far away, lay the Admiralty Pier at Dover, the one that once had the great gun which the *Illustrated London News* had imaginatively depicted in the act of blowing the tunnel entrance to pieces at the first sign of a French invasion of England through the tunnel.

Then, on hands and knees, we crawled against the pommeling wind to the very edge of the cliff, and lying on our stomachs peered straight down upon the site of the Shakespeare Cliff tunnel. I still had traces of the headache I had picked up while creeping around in the depths of the Abbots Cliff tunnel and it was a dizzying change for me now to peer three hundred feet down a sheer cliff face, but it was worth it, even though there was nothing so startling to see. Far below us lay a plateau with a couple of railway sidings on it. There were no buildings about, and certainly nothing that resembled any trace of a mine entrance. "British Railways had to build a sea wall around the whole Shakespeare Cliff area a few years ago because of the erosion from the Channel, and when we were doing that we cleaned out all the old mine workings," Adams said. "One of the last buildings to go was a shed that the old custodian of the works used to live in. His name was Charlie Gatehouse. He died about ten years ago at the age of ninety. He had worked as a timberman on both the Abbots Cliff and Shakespeare Cliff tunnels, and he took up the first sod when they dug the shaft down here. He used to tell about how one day Mr. Gladstone came down into the tunnel."

Then Adams pointed out to me exactly where the entrance to Number Two shaft had been. It lay by the third rain puddle to the left near one of the sidings. I enjoyed the thought of having its location fixed in my mind, and I believe Mr. Adams did, too. We gazed down silently. "Just imagine, if the Board of Trade hadn't stopped the works, a man might have been able to go right on to Vladivostock without getting out of his train," Adams said after a while. And he added earnestly, "But I think they'll build the tunnel yet."

Since my visit to the tunnel, the tendency of events has been to reinforce the brave hopes of Adams and his fellow pro-tunnelers. To be sure, while even the most dedicated of tunnel promoters may be prone to his black moments while pondering the nature and the effects of traditional British insularity—one of the most distinguished, Sir Ivone Kirkpatrick, the president of the Tunnel Study Group, a while ago observed with some touch of bitterness that it seemed as though "men may be flying to the moon before Britons can make a reasonable surface journey to Paris"—Britain's decision to seek full membership in the European Common Market, and the agreement of the French and British Governments to hold official talks on the construction of either a tunnel or a bridge across the Channel, have given the pro-tunnelers more solid reason for hope than perhaps has ever existed in the ranks of these visionaries in a century and a half. In the past, it was never possible for proponents of the tunnel to advance their cause with any success so long as their advocacy was not based on the prior existence of any profound change in Britain's traditional economic and strategic special and separate place in Europe, or of any change in the peculiar British sense of being an island people apart. But now such changes have taken place, or are in the process of taking place. Britain's strategic position has been profoundly altered by the advent of nuclear and rocket armaments. Her political and economic position has been as profoundly altered by the withering away of the British Empire and by the successful emergence of a new European commonwealth in the form of the Common Market. And the ancient British sense of being an island race apart seems to have been steadily eroded by a strange kind of rootlessness, partly arising out of Britain's altered place in the world, and as a general accompaniment of the intrusion of such uninsular influences as the jet airplane, commercial television, high-powered advertising, expense-account living, and the spread of installment buying. Notwithstanding all her misgivings on the subject of committing herself to abandonment of her ancient aloofness from the Continent, Britain can hardly ignore the implications of the relentless march of that process once described by the Duke of Wellington over a century ago in the heyday of the sailing ship, when he observed that Britain and the Continent were rapidly becoming joined by an "isthmus of steam."

Now that so many of the conditions that have made for England's traditional economic, military, and cultural insularity have gradually subsided, like the ancient Wealden Island that once lay in what is now the Strait of Dover, the question of connecting Britain physically to the Continent is at last in the realm of practical political possibility. In spite of all her misgivings about the abandonment of her privileged relationships with the countries of the British Commonwealth, it seems as though Britain has no choice ahead but to throw in her lot with the Common Market, which has proved itself to be such an astonishing success in its four years of existence.

Since 1958, when the special trade arrangements between the countries of the European Economic Community went into effect, up to 1960, their industrial production increased by 22 per cent, while Britain's industrial production increased only 11 per cent. And it has been estimated that by 1970 the Gross National Product of the Common Market countries will double that of 1961. This estimate does not take into account Britain's joining the Common Market, either; when she does so, as it seems she must, the Common Market boom will be a spectacular one; the member countries will then be serving a market of more than 200 million people. Precisely what Britain's entry into the Common Market would mean in terms of increased commercial intercourse between Britain and the Continent no one knows, but the increase plainly would be enormous, and considering this potentiality, proponents of the Channel tunnel are not backward in claiming that Britain's present cross-Channel transportation facilities are grossly inadequate to meet the demands ahead. They are even inadequate, the pro-tunnelers claim, for coping with Britain's present needs.

As things stand, some 8 million passengers and about 400,000 vehicles cross the Channel in a year. Of these, 3.3 million passengers and about 100,000 vehicles go by air. Most of this traffic crisscrosses the Channel in the four peak summer months and results in severe bottlenecks in the existing means of communication. (A motorist who wishes to take his car abroad either by air or sea-ferry during the peak season must book a passage some months ahead of time, and if he can't make it on the assigned date "he runs the risk," as one of the tunnel promoters has put it, "of being marooned on this island for several more months.") Even without taking into account Britain's probable entry into the Common Market, the number of vehicles crossing Britain and the Continent probably will double itself by 1965.

The Channel Tunnel Study Group people claim that neither the existing air nor sea-ferry services are equipped to handle anything like this potential load. They estimate that without construction of a tunnel, the British and French Governments, through their nationalized rail and air lines, will be obliged to spend some $90,000,000 in the next five years to replace or expand existing transport facilities if they are to keep up with the increase in cross-Channel traffic expected in that time without Britain's participation in the Common Market. As for the capacity of the tunnel, the promoters claim that all the road vehicles that crossed the Channel in 1960 could easily be carried

through the tunnel in three or four days. As for the transporting of merchandise, 11,000,000 tons of it are now being moved across the Channel in a year, most of this in bulk form—coal, for example—which it would not be practical to send through a tunnel. But of this freight, well over a million tons of nonbulk goods could, the Study Group declares, be sent by tunnel, and at about half the rates now prevailing.

Taking into account such economic advantages, the great boon to tourism that they believe a tunnel would represent, and the intangible psychological impetus that they claim a fixed link between France and Britain would give to the dream of a politically as well as economically united Europe, the pro-tunnelers believe that the construction of their railway under the Channel would be just about the greatest thing to happen to Britain in this century.

The Channel Tunnel Study Group people, as it turned out late last year, are not alone in their ambitions for a physical connection between France and Britain. Last fall, when the French and British Governments decided—on British initiative—to negotiate with each other on a fixed connection between the two countries, it became clear that a dark horse had been entered in the Channel sweepstakes with the publicizing of the new proposal for a cross-Channel bridge made by a new French company that is headed by Jules Moch, a former French Minister of Interior. The bridge proposed by the new French company would be a multipurpose affair of steel capable of carrying not only two railroad lines but five lanes of motor traffic and even two bicycle tracks. It would extend between Dover and a point near Calais. Its width would be 115 feet and its height 230 feet, allowing (as the Tunnel Study Group's proposed bridge scheme would) ample clearance for the largest ocean liners afloat. Its length would be 21 miles; it would rest on 164 concrete piles 65 feet in diameter and sunk 660 feet apart. Motorists would travel along it, without any speed limit, at a peak rate of 5,000 vehicles an hour, and an average toll of about $22.50 per car. The bridge would take between four and six years to construct, and as for the cost, that would run to about $630,000,000—or $266,000,000 more than the estimated cost of a rail tunnel. Despite some backing that the new French bridge group appears to have established for its scheme among French commercial circles, the chances are that the British Government, as representatives of a maritime nation, will have a number of objections to this plan for spanning the Channel. A principal objection—a technical one that has confounded all the Channel bridge planners from Thomé de Gamond's day onward—is the hazard to navigation within the Strait of Dover that a bridge would create. The English Channel is one of the most heavily trafficked sea lanes in the world, and considering the violent state of wind and sea within the Strait of Dover for much of the year—as well as the heavy Channel fogs—insuring safe passage between the piers of such a bridge for all the thousands of ships that pass through the Strait every year, in all weathers, would pose formidable problems even in the era of radar. Also, the Channel-tunnel advocates, who already have considered a bridge and pretty much rejected the idea because of its high cost, point to other difficulties standing in the way of the bridge idea—for example, the requirements of international law, which would make necessary a special treaty signed by all countries (including Russia) presently sending ships through the Channel before such an obstruction to navigation could be constructed; the difficulties, with all the bad weather, of keeping such an enormous structure in good repair; and the dangers of Channel gales to light European cars traversing the bridge. (The French bridge advocates claim that they could reduce the winds buffeting traffic to a quarter of their intensity by installing deflectors on the sides of the traffic lanes; to this the tunnel advocates counter that boxing cars in traffic lanes for some twenty-one miles would create a psychological sense of confinement that drivers would find far more intimidating than riding on a train under the sea.) But the main objection to the bridge is its cost. It could only be built with the help of substantial government subsidies, and the experience of the pro-tunnelers is that such subsidies are almost impossible to obtain.

Whatever the merits of the two schemes, they are certain to be considered in quite a different atmosphere now than they were back in the seventies, when, according to the observations that Sir Garnet Wolseley subsequently made to Sir Archibald Alison's scientific committee that investigated the tunnel question, "the tunnel scheme was ... looked upon as fanciful and unfeasible. It was not then regarded as having entered within the zone or scope of practical undertakings. No one believed that it would ever be made and, if mentioned, it always raised a smile, as does now any reference to flying machines as substitutes for railways." On August 28, 1961, things somehow seemed to come full circle when the London *Times*, which had started all the opposition in the press to the tunnel eighty years earlier, devoted a leading editorial to discussion of the subject of a fixed connection between France and Britain. The *Times* started out in familiar fashion for a tunnel editorial by quoting from Shakespeare's "This royal throne" speech, but then it went on to concede in stately fashion that times had changed and that "Britain must soon decide whether to leap over the wall, to become a part of Europe." The *Times* discussed the merits of the latest tunnel and bridge schemes in tones of expository reasonableness, without committing itself to either one scheme or the other, and without accusing the would-be moat-crossers, as of old, of flaunting the will of Providence. And the *Times* wound up its editorial on a meaningful note by observing, in reference to the quotations with which the editorial had been prefaced, that while Shakespeare had the first words, John Donne deserved the last:

"No man is an island, entire of itself."

To which all the tunnel dreamers, after all their years of adversity in the face of the insular British character, reasonably can say Amen.

Milton Keynes UK
Ingram Content Group UK Ltd.
UKHW030911151124
451262UK00006B/829

9 789362 517951